Bill had agre͟ed ͟to ͟help ͟me ͟with my career search and provided invaluable networking recommendations that I still pass along to candidates, even now, 12 years later. Much of his guidance seemed counter-intuitive to my new-grad-self, but I trusted and thrived in the process he laid out. Bill is a great coach because he meets you where you are at in order to help you adopt a better approach. Over the years, many have coached me in my career; Bill was the first and the one with the largest impact.

Carrie Hegenderfer
Head of Recruiting, Sands Investment Group

Bill's advice rings true and was a key element in getting my foot in the door for an interview during my job searches. Speaking from personal experience, I have trusted Bill's advice in my career moves and would highly recommend others do the same.

Steve Hannah
Chief Information Officer, Berthel Fisher Company
President, iPrism

I've found that Bill Humbert's coaching to be invaluable in job hunting. Besides giving great insight and tasks, he pushes you forward. Every time we talk, Bill ends the conversation with "How's your pipeline"?

Bruce Fryer
Executive, Technical Products

Anyone who is even remotely serious about taking their career to the next level would be doing themselves a disservice in not following Bill's guidance. I have found his methods, processes, and approaches to be enlightening and spot-on in assisting serious job search candidates wanting to advance their careers. Bill's emphasis on forward-thinking windshield driving as opposed to looking in the rearview mirror is truly refreshing—and, it is because of this that I truly am anxiously awaiting the next release in the **RecruiterGuy** series!

Tom Grondalski
Founder and Managing Partner
The Cadogan Group

Bill is *AMAZING*, in my darkest hour, and face down in the dirt he helped me get back up and dusted me off!!

Just days after being laid off Bill was there for me; a warm greeting and assured me, "this too shall pass." He wasted no time in getting to know my story, who I was and what I wanted to do in my next life. Methodically, he took me through his rock solid process that proved to be effective!

Mike Kelly
Advanced Composite Business Development
Manager, Vectorply Corporation

Bill offers the "inside track" on job seeking success tips from the recruiter's point of view, which is different than what career coaches can offer.

Amy Gleason,
Program Manager/Career Coach, University of Utah

His ability to motivate and assist individuals in their job search included skill building, confidence building and a step by step approach that took the person from feeling overwhelmed and frustrated to empowered and equipped to move forward.

Ellen Silver, LCSW
Executive Director, Jewish Family Service

The advice and support provided by Bill and the career group was essential to my successful transition after a 15 year career with the same organization. Career transitions can be tedious and the need for networking, human connection and career guidance is essential. I am thankful to have worked with Bill and maintained a long term relationship with Bill as a career advisor and is someone I continue to contact for ongoing advice. I look forward to seeing Bill's advice shared broadly through his book.

William and Susan Goldsmith

EMPLOYEE 5.0

*Employee 5.0: Secrets of a Successful Job Search
in the New World Order*

Copyright © 2018 by Bill Humbert
Published by Lisa Hagan Books

No part of this publication may be reproduced, or stored in a retrieval system, or transmitted in any form or by any means, mechanical, recording or otherwise, without the express written permission of the copyright holder.

Design: Smythtype Design
Cover image: iStock.com/Nikada

ISBN-13: 978-1-945962-90-5

Printed in U.S.A

EMPLOYEE 5.0
SECRETS OF A SUCCESSFUL JOB SEARCH IN THE NEW WORLD ORDER

Bill Humbert

LISA HAGAN BOOKS

*For my wife Linda
who has encouraged me to succeed
for over 44 years!*

Contents

Introduction 7

STEP 1   Get Started…NOW! 19

STEP 2   Exciting Employee 5.0 47

STEP 3   Here I Am! 59

STEP 4   Promote Your Career! 81

STEP 5   You Got This! 117

STEP 6   LinkedIn Literacy 125

STEP 7   Sourcing Jobs Successfully 139

STEP 8   Effective Networking! 155

STEP 9   Compelling Internships and Co-Ops ... 187

STEP 10   Impressive Interviewing 205

STEP 11   Powerful Salary Negotiation 249

STEP 12   Resigning While Resisting 281
                the Temptation of the Counter Offer

STEP 13   Onboard With Gusto! 301

Appendices... 308

Acknowledgements 348

Introduction

It is time to be honest with you—and know that I will always be honest with you! Working to find your next job is hard work! That's okay. I will be with you each step of the way.

Of course, you are asking, "What new world order?" Consider in today's world, both job seekers and companies are dependent upon the magic of technology to meet each other. Unfortunately, both will tell you job search technology is black magic. Candidates happily apply online because it is easy. You expect the instant gratification like you receive from ordering from Amazon. Then you never hear from the company. Companies like technology because they feel they do not have to put work into recruitment—like the EASY button. However, their systems drive the best candidates, YOU, away from them.

And that's the irony In this techy, uber-fast world, a few old-school techniques are the only way to blast through the screens and filters, and I'll show you how to do that here as well.

Now is time to break a new truth to you. The employment market has changed. Very, very rarely will any person remain with the same company for their entire career. This means that all employees need to become Free Agents! Yes! Just like athletes...you are responsible for your own destiny. If you leave your career to someone else, you will experience disappointment and eventually the stages of grief as a victim of downsizing.

Recovering from the grief of being laid off takes a lot out of a person. It's like a punch in the stomach that takes the air out of your lungs...and it certainly hurts. We will discuss that further in Step 1. This sense of loss takes time to overcome; and then to restart your efforts as a professional.

Consider Employment Market History. Since the end of World War II, the employment economy has crashed every eight to ten years. Everyone knows at least one person who has been laid off. Many times, you may know tens of fellow workers who were victims of a reduction in force (RIF). You may have already experienced the crushing feelings from a lay-off. Along with the coming of a recession, companies sense the economy beginning to turn. Unintentionally, they may accelerate the recession by pro-actively laying off employees. I call this the "Recruiter Economic Barometer," particularly when you see recruiters being laid off.

Companies merge and acquire other companies. During mergers and acquisitions, they falsely encourage their workforce by claiming "everyone's job is safe." Obviously, that is not true. One of the reasons companies merge is to take advantage of "synergies" acquired during the merger. That means someone is getting an opportunity to explore new jobs, i.e. riffed.

You may be asking yourself, "How do I protect my career and my income with this happening?" You will learn the steps here.

There are three groups of professionals reading this book:

1. Professionals actively searching for a new position because they have already experienced a reduction in force.

2. Professionals who have actively decided to build on their career.

3. Practice **Employee 5.0—a person who decided to take control of their career, not become dependent upon the largesse of the company to determine their growth and promotions. This professional always has a simmering search—ready to take it to boil on a moment's notice!**

Peek behind the methods of RecruiterGuy to expedite your search for your next professional position. I will lead you through this process. Keep in mind some steps are easier and others are tougher. At first, you will not call this process fun. However, if you diligently follow the process in this book, slowly you will begin to enjoy meeting many new people, some of whom may become lifelong friends—and your professional network will grow beyond your belief! By the successful end of your search, your adrenalin will be pumping and your creative juices flowing.

Do you need direction to find your way? Of course, you do. This book is your new friendly GPS built to help you control your search! Sometimes you may hear, "Recalculating!" I will never tell you to "TURN NOW!!" Since this journey is yours, you are turning to reach your goals!

Occasionally, you will hear stories about others who are in your shoes (boy, your shoes must be getting crowded...). Some stories are reinforcing great behavior. Other stories may be about people who did dumb things—don't follow their example—or you may find yourself in my next book...

> **Employee 5.0—a person who decided to take control of their career, not become dependent upon the largesse of the company to determine their growth and promotions. This professional always has a simmering search.**

In my experience career counseling, I see the frustration of jobseekers going through the search process. Because I have helped so many people find their next job, it seemed time to write a book that assists the professional jobseeker understand the processes involved and helps them be more successful. The processes in this professional edition can be used by anyone from C-Suite (CEO, CFO, CIO, etc.) to a college recruit.

Fundamentals are fundamentals: higher-level professionals simply have higher-level experience, skills, contacts, expectations and a slightly different path to their next job. The salary-negotiating tool is this book benefits professional candidates, because with their experience making positive, measurable impacts, they have more leverage. One executive who accepted a president position with a company happily reported that this salary negotiating tool enabled him to negotiate an offer that was 40 percent above what he expected the company to offer and 20 percent above what he was going to request.

Think about your search for your first job. Did someone sit down with you and prepare you for your search? Did you take a class? If you were in college and someone from the career development department tried to help you prepare for your search, did you take them seriously?

Consider the impacts of changing technology on your search. Some of the tech is helpful, particularly for research. Some of the technology only makes bad things happen faster. It is important to continue to learn the technology, explore, and understand what works for your search—and what doesn't. This book updates you to today's technology while grounding you in the fundamentals.

Speaking of technology, technical professionals tend to want to depend on technology to deliver their next opportunity to them. What prevents that from happening most of the time? It's not the technology, it is the human interface—that should resonate with you. Have you ever asked a user, "Is your computer plugged in?" See?

Humans, who do not understand that the job search is a sales process, designed systems that SCREEN OUT candidates instead of screening them in. In most companies, humans, who are either the entry level employees in Human Resource Departments (Generalizations are bad. There are expert Corporate Recruiters—and they are in the minority) or former Administrative Assistants are tasked with retrieving those resumes. **What possibly could go wrong?**

When do many people initially learn how to find a job? When they are in high school or college and a parent suggested they needed to find a job. What did most people do in that situation? They applied for a part-time position at the grocery, in retail or a fast food restaurant—and got their first job. If they were successful in those early positions, they may have been recruited to join another company. This was followed up by being recruited for their next job—and they are well into their career without truly working through a job search.

Is it any wonder that people are frustrated when they look for their next professional position, particularly if they were loyal to their first employer for 10, 20 or more years?

In 2017, I am currently working with a gentleman who began at his company as an intern. When he graduated from college as an engineer, they offered him a job. He worked for that company for 33 years. Recently, the company had a downturn; and he was laid off. ***This is the first time in his career that he has had to find a job.***

The same process they used to find their first position does not work for their next search—outside of retail. If they have been with an employer for 20 or more years and were laid off, they feel deceived and betrayed. Those feelings are so strong they are almost like a concussion—everything becomes a blur. Then the company, while truly trying to help them, will sometimes introduce them to outplacement assistance for a certain amount of time. This help occurs while a person is still trying to grasp what happened, so little of what they are taught sticks. Once they get their emotions back under control, career transition assistance may be a great help. They find that the search process they used initially no longer provides a successful process to fall back on.

Pay attention to the next sentence: The job-search process is a combination of twelve processes. Remember this.

This book has been organized by process, so you can pick it up at any time and review Steps that affect your situation. You may want to read this book from front to back like a novel—just to better understand how the processes work together. Think of your search as a manufacturing process. **What happens when you leave out a step in the manufacturing process of automobiles? You may find an automobile without wheels. Don't**

allow the wheels to fall off your job search! Follow the processes and you will succeed sooner.

Use **RecruiterGuy's Employe 5.0**, as a reference to help you work through each step of the process. Each process has its place, and each process is important to do well. These are the steps that you will work through on the way to successfully finding your next job:

- ✓ Assess your psychological acceptance process if you were laid off or otherwise feel betrayed by your last employer or board. We will discuss this important process in our first step.
- ✓ Decide your next direction or focus, and set a goal to achieve it.
- ✓ The resume-development process—and why it is **important in today's world to keep your resume updated.**
- ✓ The research/networking process (sourcing/prospecting in sales and marketing).
- ✓ The interviewing process (needs analysis in sales).
- ✓ The offer/salary negotiation process.
- ✓ The offer acceptance process (the close in sales).

- ✓ The on-boarding process when you accept the company's offer and start working.
- ✓ The retention and growth process once you begin to work at your new company (client retention in sales).

When you look at the job-search process as a series of smaller important processes, you can understand why so many books have been written on different aspects of the search. **Now it is easier to see why so many people are frustrated during a job search; They think they are "just looking for a job."**

Treat your job search as work. It is hard work. The search is worth it if you find a job where you can make positive, measurable impacts doing the things that you really enjoy. As we work through your search by using this book, you will see progress towards reaching your goals.

This television interview on *Career Transitions in Today's World* will give you a quick insight to your process moving forward. https://www.youtube.com/watch?v=nwAXmbZ1cuo&feature=youtu.be

With over 20 years of refining the job search

for hundreds of clients, I know what works. Over those years many people have demonstrated what does not work by going it their own way. I will help you get your search right while you control your destiny. Additionally, unlike many authors on the job search, I am a professional recruiter with over 36 years of recruiting experience (and still active!).

This book has been developed to help you understand the processes and begin the day-to-day steps to be successful.

Lao Tzu said, "A journey of 1,000 miles begins with a single step." It is time for you to take the first step. I will help you. If you fall, go back to the last point where you were successful and begin again. You can do it. Believe it or not, your successes will lift you.

A CFO who is conducting his or her search will need to focus on different aspects of the process than a new college graduate. A new college graduate generally is not going through the emotional trauma as someone who recently lost a job. Feel free to scan through areas that do not directly impact you. Focus on the different tasks within each process and use the checklists at the end of each step to stay on track. Use a bookmark to return to steps where you are working.

Bill Humbert • 18

RecruiterGuy.com Series

Step 1

Get Started... NOW!

If you are reading this step, you are probably one of millions of people who are in a job search or considering a search—OR, you may be Employee 5.0, trying to figure out this free agency model. Remember, surveys show that 42% of all employees are not engaged in their job! All the more reason to **become Employee 5.0 and keep your search on simmer...All The Time!** You'll stay engaged if you are always challenged, both at work and for your future career.

In either model, **the key is to become one of the tens of millions of people who are employed where they want to be employed; in the 58% of the satisfied workers.** You only need one position where you can make impacts and have fun—don't focus on the negative numbers. **Focus on finding one job.** Those who are most successful in their job searches are the ones who maintain a positive attitude and perform the fundamentals like winning athletes. Every athlete understands study, practice, execute, repeat.

The purpose of this book is to coach you to understand and work the fundamentals of a job search so well that you become the best-qualified candidate for the right job. You are competing against other well-qualified candidates who may not understand these processes. If you focus and remain positive, you can outrun the best in the field.

Just as in athletics and the performing arts, the people with the right attitudes, work ethic and proper techniques beat their competition. Job-search fundamentals are essentially the same for all professional positions—it doesn't matter if you are a CEO/CFO, a professional manager or sole contributor, a technology, accounting/finance or a sales/marketing professional. Different areas of this book focus on each level of experience but they all take the same steps to get the job.

When I offer career counseling to people, many times they seem to be afraid to take that first step into the unknown—that uncomfortable new territory; the blank white page; however, after they begin to experience some success, the adrenalin kicks in and they become comfortable with that area, but maybe hesitant about the next new area. They need help moving up the step ladder. If a step gives you problems, it gives you problems and that's why I'm here.

It is important to understand that it is not unusual for people to find change uncomfortable. As humans, many of us do not like change. Our society has been built through the years to be stable. Stability and change are opposing forces; therefore, our goal here is to help you work your way through change to get back to stability.

When you lose a job or the forces within a job become so unbearable that you decide to leave (or your spouse decides that the job is so bad for you that you become unbearable!), you will need to work through the steps of grief acceptance. This is very important for Employee 5.0 to understand too. Even the Free Agent initially expects that this new company, manager, position will propel them to their next expected level. When they are disappointed, Employee 5.0 will find themselves in a shorter period of grieving while they begin to gather their resources to search again. Every person experiences grief. Best to identify grief and then build a personal process to work through it so that you can replicate how to deal with it in the future.

The feeling of grief occurs when you lose someone or something close to you. For instance, if you lose a close family member, or even a pet, you will experience grief.

When we lost our beloved 13 year old Labrador Retriever (If you read Marley and Me by John Grogan, you knew our Kiefer) immediately after the 2010 Grammys (she hung around to see who won album of the year), we found ourselves working through the steps of grief: denial and disbelief, anger, depression and acceptance.

When you lose a job that you loved or maybe just worked at for a long time, you will need to work your way through the steps of grief. Some people really do not have a problem doing this. They may be able to embrace change more easily. If your job becomes your identity, you typically will have a more difficult time reaching acceptance.

Since 1992, my business has been a contract recruiting model where I focus my recruiting efforts on only one company at a time, my contracts generally last a minimum of 3 months, most have been extended by one or more months. When a contract ends, I enter the stages of grief. First, I don't like those feelings. Secondly, I work through all of them in a couple of hours. Then I focus on finding my next contract where I may help companies and candidates meet each other. For me, making an impact and having fun is preferable to grieving. Please understand, my process to proceed through grief moves quickly because I have more years of practice than most people.

If there is any good news, it is that you have lots of company—and I have met many people in your work shoes. You may think that you are over the anger or depression. Then, just when you expected to receive an offer, you are turned down for that position. The rejection may send you backwards into a previous step of grief. I've known people who felt like they never were going to get beyond their grief. They kept circling one or another step like they were in a whitewater hole in a river. They sometimes simply felt hopeless; however, just as in whitewater rafting, if you focus and paddle really hard, eventually you will be kicked out of the hole and continue down the river.

If you find either your anger or your depression beginning to take control over you, it is time to get some professional help. Just understand, there is no stigma attached to this; however, if you do something out of control, there is a stigma (or worse) attached to those actions. So, get some help. You don't want to hurt yourself or someone else because of an impulse generated by grief.

I also suggest you contact your creditors as soon as possible to let them know you have been laid off. They may be able to help you temporarily as you search for a job by lowering your monthly bills. Believe me, they get these calls all day long. Many companies assist with the refinancing of homes; now may be the time for you to lower your mortgage payments. Each cost cutting measure you take will help you feel more proactive and in control when you are feeling you are most vulnerable.

Your departure from your former employer may not have been your fault, but if it was, it is best just to admit it to yourself and move on to your next step. Most of us have experienced denial and disbelief during a loss. For some people, one or another of the steps will be easier based on circumstance and the emotions it generated.

If you would like to read more on the steps (or stages) of grief, go to www.google.com or www.bing.com; and search for "steps of grief" or read Elisabeth Kubler-Ross's book, *On Grief and Grieving*, the work that identified the 5 emotional stages of coming to grips with any massive change and loss.

While working your way through the stages of grief, this is the time to begin to develop your job-search strategy. Why do you want to develop your job-search strategy now? It is important to begin to claw your way out of grief. Positive action is always the best way to begin to think positively and you can do this work without putting yourself out there. It may simply be too early for that. RecruiterGuy suggests that you take advantage of this early stage by taking stock of your skills. Some consultants call this a *skills assessment.*

Here's how: Take two legal sheets. On the top of one sheet write the word "Professional." You need to use a legal sheet because it has more lines! On each line, write one of your skills or attributes. An example of a skill for a professional manager is *the ability to manage people effectively.* It may also be something as simple as *the ability to organize a desk drawer.* Examples of attributes are *honesty* and *positive mental attitude.* Fill at least every line on the front page with a skill or attribute.

Once you are satisfied with your "Professional" list, write the word "Personal" on the top of the second legal sheet. List all your personal skills and attributes. I once worked with a very talented network engineer who baked world-class desserts. We loved to see him walk into our office with his latest baked deliciousness! This network engineer would need to include *baking desserts* in his personal list. It doesn't matter how seemingly silly the skill or attribute is—list it.

One of the skills on my list is that I make the best spaghetti in Park City, Utah. (So obviously you can't use that one in Park City!) Of course, I am being facetious. You see my point. It is okay to have some fun with this.

Some skills and attributes will straddle both lists. It's fine to place them on both lists.

Now go back through your lists and put asterisks next to the skills and attributes that you enjoy doing. *For instance, as a human resource consultant specializing in the recruitment area, one of my skills is the ability to be very effective with employee relations issues. However, this is neither enjoyable nor fun for me; therefore, it does not earn an asterisk. You will not find those words together on my website. No way do I want Google to find me for those contracts!* This example illustrates how technology can work against your job search.

Once you have placed asterisks next to skills and attributes, develop a quick discussion of the 4 W's—What was the challenge? What was your response? What was the result? What did you learn? for each skill or attribute that demonstrates your ability. When your learned a lesson because of your action, it is good to add that lesson to your story; and how that lesson influenced you. ("I learned never to do that again! Instead, since then, I _____.") Just stating that a skill or attribute is a strength is not a metric. My knee-jerk reaction is to ask, "As compared to what?" Besides, people remember stories better than lists because we put ourselves into the story and relive it with you. While you are telling your story, we are picturing the events as though we were there. Tell them what you learned. Finish the story!

One of my skills as RecruiterGuy is to be very resourceful. In August 2008, I began a recruiting consulting contract with Acciona Energy NA, a renewable energy company. This was the first time in 27 years of recruitment that I was supporting a construction function within a client company.

On the first day of my contract, I went to my client's office in Chicago to meet the VP of Construction. She demonstrated that she was not pleased that Human Resources hired a contract recruiter who never recruited for construction.

The Human Resource Director introduced us as she led us to her office. Then the HR Director said, "I need to run to do something. I will return in 5 minutes." Reading the expression of the VP Construction, I thought, "The little lamb is being led to slaughter..."

Employee 5.0

The VP Construction sat down with her back to me (really a bad body language sign). Then she looked over her shoulder and said, "You have never recruited for Construction?"

I replied, "No."

She replied, "Well good luck with this!"

My response? I laughed (well it was not a belly laugh because I did not want to die). She asked, "Why are you laughing right now?"

I replied, "I have been recruiting since 1981. Do you know how many times I have heard that?"

She said, "No?"

"Almost every single new client. My performance is so strong about two years later I receive a call—'Hey Bill, when are you breaking free of your current client?'"

She said, "We'll see!"

Within three weeks, I set up five personal interviews on-site and my client hired three of those candidates for three positions we had open. How was I successful so quickly? I used the skills that I developed and honed over the years to source candidates, and applied them to this new field. In the process, I discovered a new job board for my client to use in future construction candidate searches.

Oh, and two years later, they called to see if I could break free from my current client to help them find more qualified candidates for their continued growth.

It is best that you are prepared going into an interview having already rehearsed up the best stories that demonstrate your abilities. Most of your competitors will not prepare this way. They wait until they are put on the spot. Then hope their brain cooperates by giving them the best story—but it doesn't always happen. How many times have you reflected on a conversation and thought, "I wish I would have said…"

Why is this exercise important? There are many reasons why you need to be serious about this work:

- ✓ You need to review these skills and attributes to prepare yourself for your interviews.

- ✓ You need to be able to demonstrate that these are skills that produce measurable results.

- ✓ It is important for you to understand your value to a new company.

- ✓ This exercise helps you through the other stages of grief and may be enough to propel you through them. These stories create the foundation to renew your self-worth.

- ✓ You may decide that this is a great time to go in a completely different career direction where you are using the skills you really enjoy—possibly even starting your own business. Have fun at work. What a concept!

I was once interviewed for a presentation on "Effective Networking to Your Next Position!" The freelance writer honored me by telling me that two years before, she was going through a particularly tough job search. We spoke after one of my presentations. During our conversation, we discussed the job-search process and aspects of it that she had not considered. Because of our conversation, she changed her search completely and now is enjoying her new career in sales. She is using the same relationship-building skills that she had used previously, but now she is having more fun and generating more income.

> **Place a bookmark in this page and complete the task of developing stories that demonstrate your skills before continuing further.**

It is important in the early stages of a job search to be task-focused. Every task completed is a success. As we move forward in this book, create a checklist of tasks so you may happily check off completed ones. Right now, success in any process is important to your self-worth and helps you build a positive attitude. As we move forward, the processes will require more strategic skills and sometimes multitasking.

Many times, once you get past your denial, you find yourself angry at your situation, your job loss, your former manager, your former company and/or executives, yourself, or all the above. Anger is fine if you work through it. Revenge can be a strong motivator. However, the revenge needs to be directed toward a positive conclusion, not towards an individual or a company. Be careful with revenge because it can become all-encompassing. Use its power to find your next job where you can make positive, measurable impacts. Then, when you are wildly successful at your next company, you can briefly look back and say to yourself proudly, "See!"

Once you work your way through your anger, you may find yourself depressed. Many times, the loss of a job brings feelings that you are somehow worthless. Just understand that companies do not have good track records when it comes to laying off the right people. You may have been an "impact performer" in the wrong place at the wrong time. If you cannot work through depression by yourself, seek professional assistance. Understand that many people experience depression during this process. You are not alone in these feelings. Generally, many people cry while they are discussing their feelings with me. My reaction is that it is important to let them cry. It can help them work their way through their situation—kind of a cleansing. Once the crying is done, it's back to work with a sense of urgency.

Obviously, this is the time to work on more positive activities to prepare for networking. You will need to know whom to call and their phone numbers. This gives you a track to work every day. With the ease of creating spreadsheets and expanding them as needed, I recommend that you create a spreadsheet with four columns: name, phone number, where the person works and how you know him or her. (This may be a referral from someone else.) You can also use paper or even a whiteboard.

List 350 names on those spreadsheets. It seems like a lot of names and phone numbers. But when you begin to network, you will need at least that many contacts. They do not need to be friends. The list may contain family, friends, acquaintances, neighbors, pastor/rabbi/minister/spiritual mentor, parents of your children's friends, former peers at other companies, former managers, alumni from your high school and college(s), your banker, attorney and real estate agents. Ask your family to look at your list. They may remember people that you forgot. You do not have to create this list in one sitting. As a matter of fact, it is good practice to add to it consistently.

If you are a CEO, CFO, CTO, CIO, CMO, CHRO, etc., your list needs to contain the names of consultants and account executives that have sold or tried to sell you their products or services. Obviously, these people have connections to people in your field at your level.

Depending upon their products or services, they may know influential corporate board members.

If you are an experienced manager or sole contributor, your list should contain people who are in sales and previous peers and managers, as well as those former classmates from high school and college. Anyone can know anyone and may be influential in helping you meet the right person.

If you are graduating from college and are new to the workforce, you also have access to a network of names in the workforce. Attend the on-campus and local career fairs. Talk with the Alumni office to find which Alumni work at companies that you are targeting. Contact people where you worked on an internship. Have you discussed your search with your friends? Do you know what their parents' professions are?

If you have not already created a profile on www.LinkedIn.com and have begun inviting people you know to your LinkedIn network, you need to begin working on that now. We will discuss LinkedIn in depth later. However, since it is a powerful networking tool, it is important to update your profile as you move through your career—not just when you "need" to look for your next position. You can find people listed by companies and by educational affiliations (high schools and colleges). You may also join LinkedIn groups that are tied to your industry and associations that are tied to your fields. LinkedIn has become a very valuable tool for both business development and job searching. There is more information on LinkedIn in **Step 5: LinkedIn Literacy (page 117)**.

Below is a sample of a Networking Spreadsheet:

NETWORKING TO A JOB SPREADSHEET (SAMPLE)

Name	Phone	Company	How I Know
John Doe	435-555-2045	Ability Co.	Neighbor
Jane Doe	435-555-2391	Honest Insurance	Co-Worker
Irving Milliken	319-555-9345	Accountant Inc.	Jane Doe

This is simply an example. Many professionals have a way to create a contact spreadsheet that fits their professional needs. Sales professionals may use their own contact software, such as Act! to track and add new contacts. Both existing spreadsheets or a contact management software system may already have names and contact information in them that is valuable in this process.

Before proceeding to the next task, really focus on developing your list of names. This list is very important for tracking and setting goals for your networking activities. **You need the base of 350 names because people who refer you to someone else are your most valuable commodity during a job search. Why? As compared to "cold calls" to people you don't know, calls to someone who was referred to you by someone else is known as a "warm referral."** I challenge you to grow your list as you network to 500 names of potential contacts! You will regain confidence and accelerate your job search. Additionally, when a contact is one of 500, there is less pressure on you to get positive results from each person. Then you are more relaxed in your conversation with them. The practice of exceeding expectations works in jobs and in job searches.

Did you notice there is no column for email address? That omission is intentional. Your contact needs to be over the phone or in person. Email creates contact problems:

1. Many times, company email servers shuttle outside emails to the spam folder.

2. You don't always know they were read.

3. Busy people may want to contact you, but your email gets lost in the sea of emails they receive.

And the result is that you become frustrated that people do not respond. At this point in your search, the last thing you need is more frustration. Emails are great later, after you have established contact and are communicating. That's when you'll make it through the spam filter and, at that point, you may be sending updated resumes and letters. Often, your contacts will forward those documents to the "gate keepers"—human resources—or the person with the hiring power. They may even forward it to competitors where they have friends and colleagues—good humans are like that.

Some professionals question whether the US Mail is sufficient for sending your resume. The problem with the mail is the perception that you are "behind the times." If you are an executive, not mid-level professional, who hears about an open executive position, and wish to differentiate yourself without networking, you may try another tack. Overnight your resume to the CEO via FedEx with a cover letter that legitimately details why they should interview you. It is best to be able to mention who informed you about their need for a new or replacement executive. It is important that the referral is willing to discuss why it is appropriate that the executive spend their valuable time with you. It is best if that person calls the CEO directly instead of you. This method builds credibility for you.

Given the practice of promoting positive activity during negative times, if you find yourself in a funk because of your situation, now is the time to begin to list your accomplishments over the past five years. This list is different than the skills assessments in that you are focused on your professional impacts. If you are feeling depressed, it may be difficult to develop this list. That is not at all unusual. Why? It is difficult for our minds to switch from negative to positive—and from positive to negative. This is the reason you need to focus on a positive activity when you do not feel positive. **Focus on positive results to work through the negative feelings.**

One place to look for your impacts is your old annual or board reviews. Create paper copies to store in your home files. If you wait until you depart a company to look at your reviews, it is too late. They just deleted you from their system. All professionals should invest in themselves by storing and reviewing their annual reviews. Shouldn't you review not only your impacts? Isn't best to review where you needed improvement; and determine how far you improved? **Employee 5.0 professionals use these reviews both as metrics to determine where they are on track to meet their goals and to determine where they need additional attention and effort.**

Accomplishments in former positions can be large money-saving endeavors or smaller achievements. A sales professional may have exceeded their quota for the past three years. A manufacturing operations leader may have used a lean process improvement to lower costs and increase productivity. A commercial banker may have several years when every loan was profitable and closed on time.

For practice, use action verbs to describe the activity. Never begin an accomplishment with the words "have or had." **Always begin a story or resume sentence with an action verb** (See Appendix A on page 308). There are also lists of action verbs on the Internet, so simply type "action verbs" into a search engine like Google or Bing to find potential verbs that fits your experience. **Here are some examples: designed, developed, managed, created, saved, solved, recruited, mentored, piloted, audited, introduced, negotiated, motivated, purchased, analyzed, sold, assessed and organized.**

This is an example of how to write a story about your accomplishments. Note the elements— The 4 W's—What was the challenge? What was your response? What was the result? What did you learn?—"as a result I now..." or "now I've changed the way I approach that challenge...."

As the recruiting manager of a startup telecommunications firm in 1995, I discovered that our paper process to open new jobs was unwieldy. We were too dependent on people staying at their desks to approve the openings. Additionally, we never knew where jobs were in the approval process. I noticed that our help desk professional was using Lotus Notes shareware to develop applications for our customer service group.

Since applications are the automation of a paper process, I approached the help desk professional to ask if she would be interested in teaming with me to develop an automated process to track job requisitions. She said she was interested. I then approached her manager to get his approval for her to work on this project during her unproductive time.

We worked on this project part-time over six months. Deb did a great job! We ended up developing an applicant-tracking system/human resource information system in 1995 using Lotus Notes shareware. It did not cost our startup any money. The system was robust enough to be used as the company grew from 400 employees to 8,000 employees.

A positive mental attitude is crucial during a job search. In his book *How to Stop Worrying and Start Living*, Dale Carnegie had wonderful advice. Ask yourself, "What is the worst possible outcome of this situation? Once that is on the table, work to improve on it." This is a great book and one worth reading, especially if you are feeling stressed. It helped me through a particularly tough patch early in my recruitment career.

It is generally good to find something positive to do during this period while you are angry or depressed. Have you considered volunteering? This is a great outlet. It gets you out of the house. You are meeting people, contributing with your skills and sometimes helping people who are in a much worse predicament than you are. Generally, the people who receive the benefit of your service are genuinely grateful for everything that you do. These positive actions reinforce your sense of worth; and give back to your community.

Who do we find on the boards and in the volunteer ranks of nonprofits? Usually, business people accept those positions. It's a great way to get noticed and at the same time feel more worthwhile. Doing something that is positive is far more productive than sitting at home depressed. When we discuss networking, your volunteer work is a great base because you are demonstrating that you are not only concerned about yourself, you are also concerned about others. It also gives you possible discussion points during interviews. And remember your contacts? It adds names to your list.

Occasionally, I have seen people have such a great experience in their volunteer work that they decide to accept a position with the nonprofit; and they make contributions to its success as a fulltime employee.

None of this will happen in a flash, but you will know when you reach the first level of acceptance. Listing all your skills and attributes and network of contacts will help you feel your power. You'll know when it's time to move forward in a positive direction. You may have setbacks as you work through these steps, but now that you have a greater understanding of yourself and this process, you'll work through in ever-shorter times. Once you reach acceptance, it is time to get out and prepare to interview.

Congratulations!

Now you are in a positive position to take the next steps. Let's move forward and treat this search like your job. Get up in the morning. Take a shower. Dress professionally as you did for work—or possibly more professionally as a consultant or sales professional. You need to work at least eight hours every day on some aspect of your search, including volunteer work. RecruiterGuy will continue to help you take each day at a time.

Let's review your "To-Do List" before moving on:

> ✓ Take stock of your skills in your professional and personal lives **using Descriptive Impact Verbs** (Refer to Appendix A).

- ✓ Develop a quick discussion of The 4 W's—What was the challenge? What was your response? What was the result? What did you learn from your actions—Good and Bad!

People remember stories, not lists.

- ✓ **Develop a list of your positive, measurable impacts.** Create a problem-your response-result around each impact, and what you learned. If you still have old annual reviews, read through them for impacts that you may have forgotten. The additional benefit is the annual review is in the eyes of the reviewer, not your eyes.

- ✓ **Develop a list of a minimum of 350 names of family, friends and acquaintances,** neighbors, former peers/managers in your last company and previous companies, high school and college alumni, neighbors, pastor/rabbi/spiritual mentor, banker, attorney and real estate agents. Look up their contact information in your address book, LinkedIn, the phonebook or search for them with Google or Bing on the Internet. Remember, if you know where they work, you may simply call the company's general phone number and ask for them. If you are asked why you are calling, reply, "It's a business matter" or "We're friends." (Best be friends if you use that method. Not good form for them to reply, "Who?")

- ✓ Join LinkedIn and invite everyone you feel can help you and that you can help somewhere. **Remember, it is important to give back to other people.** When people accept your invitation, go through their network and see if there may be contacts that you forgot to enter on your list. This action may help you remember additional people to add to your spreadsheet. Remember that people know other people — and LinkedIn is a great example of how it can work.

Now it's time to work on your next step. Remember to focus on each step and do it well. Some steps will take longer than others. Treat your search as Your Business. It is good to use the above list to check off completed steps. **You are**

building a strong foundation that will improve your job search. All the work you have performed in this step is preparation. Preparation for creating your resume, for your "Here I Am!" speech, for networking, and for interviewing. Isn't the Boy Scout motto, "Be Prepared!"

Work very hard to maintain a positive mental attitude. Your attitude will determine how quickly you find a job. Remember Winston Churchill during the darkest hours of the Battle of Britain in World War II — "Neva Give Up!"

Remember your bookmark? This is a great place to use it if you need to complete these tasks.

STEP 2
===

Exciting Employee 5.0

Employee 5.0s are professionals who do not accept that their company should have the sole control of their career. These professionals keep their search on simmer, so they can turn it up to BOIL instantly. In today's world they are sometimes referred to as "Passive Candidates." There are far more **Employee 5.0** members than most people realize. This concept is in wide use today—it just did not have a name…until now.

According to Intuit CEO, Brad Smith* during an earnings call in May 2017, approximately 34% of American workers are a 1099 independent contractor[1]. Additionally, we need to factor in travel nurses, many sales professionals, most executives, athletes, actors/actresses, TV hosts/news

---

1*http://money.cnn.com/2017/05/24/news/economy/gig-economy-intuit/index.html

professionals, musicians, singers, and others. Rarely do Executive Directors of non-profits remain for their entire career—unless they were the Founder. Therefore, you will even see Employee 5.0 show up in nonprofits—executive directors look for better opportunities to grow their career, especially when they are successful attracting donations for their current charity.

Employee 5.0 is a professional who accepts and welcomes change, either inside their company or outside their company. Their prime interest is to do a great job for their company; and receive the appropriate recognition for a job well done. They accept they need to prove themselves in their current positions. Then, they expect the appropriate promotion to make greater contributions and grow their career.

Keeping these professionals in mind, you may be an Employee 5.0 who forgets to keep your search on "simmer." Possibly, you did not quite know you were Employee 5.0 because you didn't have a name for it. Now you do as you look to improve your position in your current company or elsewhere.

How do you "become" Employee 5.0 and take advantage of the new model?

The first step is to decide you will always keep your search turned on, not actively, subtly. Keep your ears open all the time. I have recruited candidates in airports on multiple occasions. Restaurants, subway cars, and truly any place people gather are places where my ears are tuned to conversations. If someone overhears your conversation and decides they want to chat, open yourself to the conversation. Remember the old saying, "Talk is cheap"? It applies right here. If there is no interest, just say so, thank the person...and move on. It may be wise to exchange numbers for your contact grid of the future. You just never know when that call may come unexpectedly; or, you may decide to initiate the conversation.

This is the time, while you are working, that you take calls from recruiters that you trust. How do you learn which recruiters to trust? It does take some time, but over time you can determine if their interests represent a win-win for you and them. Many recruiters strictly are interested in their income, not your career. Look for those rare recruiters who will listen to your description of an ideal position. Then they will call you with opportunities that you may want to explore. Feel free to help them focus on your professional desires and needs (including compensation).

Where do you find Professional Recruiters instead of "recruiters"? Talk to friends in your industry or field. Your pretense is that you are interested in recruiters who may help you fill openings at your company.

Sometimes my candidates hear from me about their perfect position a year later. Every single time, that person interviewed and was offered a significant increase that they accepted—that's an Employee 5.0.

As you can tell Employee 5.0 is an attitude that becomes a habit.

As an employee, are you happy with your annual 2% raise? Would you prefer to provide a nicer lifestyle for your family? Your decision is yours, not mine.

If you are interested in providing a nicer lifestyle, please complete this step. If you simply want a job, you may skip the secrets in this step and move directly to Step 3.

Secret 1. You have control over your career.

Many people just float through their careers wherever the tides of the company take them. It is not in the best interests of your manager nor your company for you to become Employee 5.0. They are perfectly happy where you are. If you decide to move within your company or outside of your company, your current manager needs to recruit someone to fill your shoes. Am I correct? Just examine your personal career. Have you ever applied internally for an attractive position and were told, "Let's finish this project first?" Then the position is filled with someone else because that manager needs their position filled.

Employee 5.0 is focused on their career. They make positive, measurable impacts and as the result, have fun working. Once they establish their reputation as a top performer inside a company, they begin to plan their next move. If they like working at their company, they will try there first. If the move does not happen within their company, they will widen their search and quietly network outside their company.

Companies do not always recognize the value of the talent in their organizations. One reason is they will sometimes promote someone who is a great sole contributor to manager, thinking the skills translate to management. Their skills as a sole contributor work against them as a manager. Therefore, they view top performers in their organization as a threat to their management position. This is the reason talented new professionals are sometimes caught up in reductions in force—remove the threat. Once you realize that you report to this type of manager, it is time to leave that manager as soon as possible.

Secret 2. Develop a mentor relationship with a successful executive

This executive is someone who recognizes your skills/experience/future promise and is willing to meet you once every month or two to discuss your current contributions within the company. The relationship is strong enough that you will follow their suggestions, including registering for a professional MBA program, if they feel you would benefit. They are the person who may suggest that your next position in the company will open soon; and possibly introduce you to the manager as a potential candidate. Rarely, but sometimes, they may suggest that now is the time for you to find a new position outside of the company. Possibly they will get wind that your current manager is feeling threatened with your performance. When you receive that advice, turn your search to boil immediately!

Secret 3. Volunteer for the "Dirty Jobs"

The dirty jobs are the jobs that no one else wants. Your fresh look at the project may provide you an opportunity to successfully complete that project in a way that builds your reputation as a person who gets things done. Pick projects that have the potential to build revenue or save money. Added complexity and low expectations for success create low bars that can build your reputation when you succeed and exceed baseline expectations. These are situations where the bar for success is very high, but few people believe you can possibly succeed. You believe you will succeed. Then build a winning strategy.

Several years ago, a Director approached me. He had an important project that would take a year to complete. I was surprised and honored that he asked me to lead this project. On the other hand, it was going to be very difficult. I asked my peers to ask their executives if they felt anyone could be successful with that project. They all responded, "No way!"

After receiving the responses, I told my Director that I would be happy to accept the project. The expectations of success were so low, what did I have to lose? We exceeded the aggressive goal by 15%! All the people who participated in that project benefitted from our success.

These are steps to determine if you should tackle the "dirty job."

1. Examine the project.

2. Determine the possibility of success for yourself.

3. Ask leaders how important the project is for the company.

4. Make the decision.

What is the upside if you succeed in cleaning up this dirty job? You build a reputation of success within the company. Every company has dirty jobs. Sometimes, when you examine the project, you may find the process is no longer required. The process may currently still be performed manually, but there is a better way to perform the task automatically using current technology. If that is the case, it is best to build consensus with the leadership prior to eliminating the process.

Employee 5.0 leverages this success to build their career, inside or outside their company. Over the years, many of my successful introductions were professionals who found their perfect job within their company. Unfortunately, their current company would not give them the promotion, so they decided to look outside.

Who benefits more? Professionals who stay in the same company for a long period? Or, people who move about every 5 years? Generally, every time a professional changes companies, they are rewarded with more money to make the change. Obviously, if you own equity in your current company, you need to take the consequences of your departure into account. There is a balance. Ensure you make positive, measurable impacts in your company prior to moving outside your company. You want to be able to demonstrate growth...not escape.

Employee 5.0 maintains a positive attitude while keeping their job search on simmer.

Utilize your Employee 5.0 positive attitude to build your Employee 5.0 habit! With your positive attitude and positive results, other people are attracted to you. They want to join your projects because those successes will also benefit their careers. Your successes build your expectation of success. Expectation of success leads to more success.

Let's review your "To-Do List" before moving on:

1. Are you still growing your skill and experience lists? These lists need to be dynamic. Many times, professionals develop a new

skill or make an impact within their company. These skills and impacts need to be noted in your skills/impacts lists. I suggest that you add them when the skill is developed, or impact is made. Organize them by the year. This enables them to be brought up and discussed during an annual review. Managers tend to struggle with these conversations because most managers do not develop a habit of writing them down. By the way, these discussions are great practice for interviewing.

2. Focusing on those skills you do well and enjoy doing, have you built your stories to illustrate each skill? The First Step certainly demonstrates the importance of building stories where you discuss The 4 W's—What was the challenge? What was your response? What was the result? What did you learn?

3. Have you added to your list of positive, measurable impacts—with the stories?

4. Have you developed a spreadsheet with a minimum of 350 names for networking? Is the list up-to-date?

5 Do you have a LinkedIn profile? Have you opened your privacy so people outside your network may view your profile—and others who are connected to you?

6 Are you adopting the Employee 5.0 positive attitude?

If you need more time to complete your To-Do items, pause here. Work on them now.

Propel Your Career—AND Your Income Forward as Employee 5.0!

We Got This!

Let's get started on "WHAT'S NEXT? 'HERE I AM!'"

STEP 3

What's Next? "Here I Am!"

Whether you are in an active job search or are Employee 5.0 (with your career search always on simmer!) think of your search as a new adventure. Enjoy your hunt! Don't get swallowed up in the perceived enormity of it; simply stay focused on your very next task. As you are successful in each, you are moving in the direction of success to reach your final goal—a new job or possibly even starting your own business using the skills you've developed working for others.

In the new world order, everyone should be Employee 5.0! Too much of your work life is out of your control. Can you control Executive decisions? Not unless you are the one making the decisions. Can you control Mergers and Acquisitions? No, unless you are the person responsible for the decision. Do you control downsizing? Probably not.

What can you control? Your career goals, your actions, your decisions—and hopefully one of those is to keep your search for a growth position on the front burner.

What you can control are your day to day responsibilities, strategic responsibilities, and keeping your search moving forward. I am teaching you the new reality—there is virtually no more job security anywhere—and how to address it. From this point forward, my assumption is everyone understands the importance of Employee 5.0 as a practice. The employment world has changed; change with it.

Since 1994, when I have spoken to organizations nationwide on the "Secrets of a Successful Job Search," I asked those gathered the following question: "What elements make you happy when you are working?" Generally, there are many responses, including compensation or benefits. Think about it. There are many elements that can make you happy—great peers, great managers, fun projects, great benefits/pay, cool challenges, self-fulfillment, etc. When you boil these down to the base elements, what are the things that combine with others to make you happy? Doesn't it come down to, "Am I making positive, measurable impacts?" and "Am I having fun doing so?"

If you are making positive, measurable impacts and having fun doing so, you will make the impacts necessary to earn what you need. The feeling that I would love to see you achieve at work is this: "I am making such great impacts and having so much fun, I can't believe they are paying me, too!" You can reach that level of satisfaction. That may seem far away right now. It is attainable when it is your goal. Along with the work to find your new position, this is the theme that is interwoven throughout this book. If you are conducting a job search, why not find something that you love to do—and be paid well to do it?

Let's review where you should be now in your search. You are probably three to five days into your search while reading this book. You have completed your skills assessments, probably even made some additions to your skills and attributes after chatting with people you know. Sometimes family, friends, co-workers, and managers can see things in you that you don't recognize until they point them out. Therefore, it is good to ask other people for their feedback.

You worked a little on the list of examples that demonstrate successful use of those skills, but gave up after a while because you were frustrated that you are in this situation and are anxious "to get started." Remember, this is a process. To win championships, individuals or teams need to perform the fundamentals well. How do they perform the fundamentals well? They practice them to perfection every single day. Chances are that you may have never worked on some of these fundamentals during job searches. Let's practice and do them well!

I have voluntarily helped hundreds of people succeed in finding their next job through this process. Have you ever snow skied? When you were learning how to ski, did you immediately go to the expert slopes? Probably not (unless you were a fearless young boy or girl!). You worked your way up to them. It was a process that involved success and failure. The successes built your confidence to try the next, more difficult slope. That's the process we are growing here. Build some success somewhere. Use that new confidence to go to the next step. **Remember, a positive mental attitude is crucial in the job-search process.**

Going back to your skills assessment, it is very important to develop the examples that demonstrate your success with that skill or attribute. After jotting down some examples, get away from them overnight. The next morning, you may remember better examples for some of those skills or attributes. During the interviewing process, I refer to them as the "Wish I Would Have Saids!" Write your stories and practice them. Many times, this process will help you remember even better stories to tell (that you write and practice).

All of this is important preparation prior to your interviewing process, so focus doing the best job you can. Your search success, income and happiness depend on it. You will notice that occasionally I will reinforce process tasks that I mentioned in previous steps.

I do this because of my experience working with people. It's not unusual to get further down the road while career counseling and have someone tell me, "Well, I really haven't focused on that yet..." **Think of RecruiterGuy as the little guy sitting on your shoulder in a business suit, with legs dangling and rooting you on—and coaching in your ear that you need to do a better job on your list of potential networking names or skills or accomplishments or *whatever.***

You began your list of 350 people and then gave up after the first 53 names because it seemed like there were too many names to dredge up. Most people have impacted the lives of 350 people in some fashion, so ask your immediate family who you've forgotten from your list and add them. Did you remember your friends and acquaintances in your neighborhood? How about neighbors in former neighborhoods? If both members of a couple are working, you can add both names. (Never assume that married/significant other couples talk about everything!) Where have you volunteered? Who do you remember from those experiences? What sales professionals do you know? They truly understand the networking process. Their livelihoods depend on networking. Go to your high school and college alumni associations. See who you forgot to add from there. Remember that it's not just your class; you knew people in the classes before you and after you. You have your high school or college in common with them. Generally, people still feel warmth toward others who had similar experiences, whether in school or work. That is the reason you see work alumni groups on LinkedIn. We are now focusing on your "warm" contacts who have something in common with you. I will teach you how to work through cold calling to warm referral calling.

While you are working on those tasks, I have another question that I ask during my "Secrets of a Successful Job Search" presentation. How many of you, in some part of your life, are involved in sales? If you agree, raise your hand. Invariably a few people will not raise their hand. I suggest that I was not asking if they made their living in sales. The key phrase is "in some part of your life." I ask again, "How many of you, in some part of your life, are involved in sales?" Upon reflection, more people raise their hand.

There is always that one person who insists they are not involved in sales. So, I ask them, "Have you ever tried to sell a child on the idea of finishing their meal or going to bed?" They shake their head "No." I ask them if they ever tried to sell a friend on the idea of going to a ball game, movie or other activity. They still say, "No." I persist nicely and ask, "To clarify my thinking, have you ever tried to sell a co-worker on a better way to do things?" Generally, they have gone this far down the path and don't want to admit they are wrong, so they say, "No."

Then I ask, "So what I am hearing (pause) is that you are trying to sell me on the idea that you are not involved in sales, is that correct?" Everyone else thanks their lucky stars that they raised their hand. **And We Are ALL Involved in Sales Daily.** "Influencing" people is the same as selling them. You are Selling an Idea. **In your career search, you are selling hiring managers that you are the best qualified candidate for their position.**

The process to find a job is a sales process. People who realize this are successful more quickly than those who don't. The good news is that we have gotten you this far before we had to tell you this information—and you have built some belief and success through your early tasks, if you completed them.

The spreadsheet below demonstrates that the Sales Process and Job Search Process mirror each other perfectly.

Sales Process	Job Search Process
Identify Need	Need New Job
Create Solution	Create Resume/LinkedIn
Source Potential Clients	Source Potential Employers
Needs Analysis	Interview
Proposal	Offer
Due Diligence	Drug/Background/References
Cost Negotiation	Compensation Negotiation
Close Sale	Close Hiring Manager
Delivery of Product	Start Date
Product Training	Orientation
Retaining Clients	Employee Retention and Growth

Every step of the Job Search matches the Sale Process without even one deviation. Every step matches without even one deviation. Now, if we could only help companies understand that the Recruiting Process also mirrors the Sales Process perfectly, everyone would be happier—and more successful!

Watch this television interview that discusses the Job Search Sales Process (and you will see an insect walking behind Eliza that was also intrigued with the interview)—https://www.youtube.com/watch?v=JIuzaWPkjwE&feature=youtube.

Now that you understand you are in a sales process, let's treat it as such. One of the first things new sales professionals are taught is how to set and attain goals.

Let's keep in mind the metrics over the past 40 years, tracked by the Career Transition industry.

1. If you speak with two networking contacts per week, it will take you a year (on average) to find a job.

2. If you speak with 10 new networking contacts per week, it will take you 6 months (on average) to find a job.

3. If you speak with 20 new networking contacts per week or 4 per day, it will take you 90 days (on average) to find a job.

Decide on your next career and set a goal. When you set goals, it is important to consider all the elements of a goal. This is a key step for Employee 5.0. I recommend that you use the word **-SCAMPS-** to remember the required elements to succeed:

> **S—Specific/Strategy:** Your goal needs to be **specific** for you to visualize successfully reaching your goal. Once you visualize it, you need to create a **strategy** to attain your goal.

In your job search, your goal could be, "By Jan. 2 (or whatever the date is 90 days out), I will be working as a (n) _____ with _____ Company. I will get this position by contacting at least 20 new networking contacts per week to discuss my background." This is a realistic goal if the position could be available by then. You also give yourself a way of measuring your activity. You have set your goal to find a job; and your strategy is to network your way there.

> **C—Challenging:** Challenging goals spur you to action. You are excited to work on them. Your brain loves a challenge!

In this example, you have set the goal of finding a job in 90 days by networking with 4 people per day. This is challenging because it requires 4 conversations, not messages left. Besides finding a job in 90 days is also a nice challenge that requires focus and work (and belief).

A—Attainable: While they need to be challenging, you must also believe that you can successfully attain goals. Otherwise you will not work to succeed because your brain says, "You know you can't do this!"

If you set a goal of finding a job in 5 days, unless you were successful doing so in the past or have one lined up already, you probably will not believe you can make that happen. However, if you set a goal to find a job in 90 days and have a proven strategy, your mind is willing to go for it.

M—Measurable: The steps to completing a goal must be measurable. It is important to know every day the steps that you need to take toward achieving your goal. If the goal is not measurable, how will you determine your required hourly/daily tasks?

By creating a strategy of talking with 20 networking contacts per week (4 per day), you can measure your activity. This gives you a path that needs to be followed. If you do not speak with 20 contacts one week (possibly because of interviews), you need to step up your networking activity the following weeks to catch up.

P—Public: You need to let people who support you know that you set the goal. They will ask for progress reports. This step provides accountability. Do not bother telling people you know will throw cold water on your goals. How would that help you? Talk with positive people.

S—Set End Date: Once you have created a goal, it is important to set your completion date. This step, tied to the measurable steps enables you to determine what actions you need to take daily to achieve your goal. This second S is the bungee cord that ties all the steps together with the first S.

I learned how to set goals at DeMatha High School in Hyattsville, Maryland. As a college sophomore on April 6, 1969, I read that Greyhound would take passengers from Washington, DC to Los Angeles in 5 days. My thought? "If Greyhound can do it…I can do it!" This television interview discusses how we succeeded—https://www.youtube.com/watch?v=9dVOYNkMWxE

Following **SCAMPS**, both Employee 5.0 and the active job searcher now have a path to successfully follow.

Few things irritate me more while working a career fair than a candidate who approaches me and says, "So what do you have open?" My response always is the same: "What do you want to do?" During a job search, it is important to be able to verbalize your job-search goal. Don't fear rejection. Most people want to help you!

It's time for the bookmark again. Take some time to internalize what I just said and develop your first goals. One of your goals might be to complete the tasks that have already been assigned within the next two days. If you begin having success, it is fine to set more aggressive goals—just be realistic and understand that more aggressive goals require more aggressive work and results.

Let us now work on your list of accomplishments in your jobs over the past five years. You have already listed your skills and attributes and developed stories that demonstrate success using them. You created your accomplishment list. Now list the most recent accomplishments first and the earlier accomplishments further down the list. Put them in the descending order of accomplishing them. If you still have employee reviews, you can use them to jog your memory. If you were very astute, you may have developed a list of your accomplishments every year prior to your annual review.

Now that we have much of the preparation done, the process will move more quickly. Hopefully you have made some progress working through the steps of grief—watch out for that denial one! When I hear someone protest they are not in denial when I did not even bring it up in our conversation, should I feel they may still be in denial? My sense is, "yes."

Because we are in a sales process, now we are going to work on the first of your marketing pieces—your "Here I Am!" speech. It's time to get your creative juices flowing and have some fun with this task. Your "Here I Am!" speech is also called an elevator speech or one-minute commercial. This is the beginning of branding yourself as a candidate or a professional. The more successful candidates are the ones who do a good job differentiating themselves. Your "Here I Am!" speech is not something you can memorize; it is something you feel. You'll know you have hit it on the head when it feels good to you when you repeat it. Let's work on building it right now. **What are the base elements of a "Here I Am!" speech?**

- ✓ **Talk about your experience and**

talents/impacts. It's important to discuss why you are passionate about that type of work. This is a key differentiator for you. Importantly, your face lights up when you speak about something that you do where you are passionate.

✓ **Discuss briefly why you are in this situation of looking for a job.** Relax. My feeling is that the recession in the early 1990s was the first white-collar recession. The dot-bomb recession from 2000 to 2002 was strongly a professional and technical recession. Then the recession of 2008 until 2012 impacted everyone; therefore, everyone knows someone who was laid off or otherwise lost a job and did not deserve to be out of work. It has no stigma attached unless you were terminated for cause.

✓ **Talk about what you would like to do next.** Below is an example of a "Here I Am!" speech that an engineer gave me after 9/11 when his company had to lay off several hundred professionals.

✓ **Ask the following question**—*Who would you suggest that I speak with next?* Many professionals ask, "Do you have any jobs?" As a Recruiter, even I say, "No." as a knee jerk response because I do not know you well enough yet. Then you are done. Best to ask to plug into their network.

After the terrorist attacks on the World Trade Center and the Pentagon in 2001, a company in Cedar Rapids was forced to lay-off several hundred engineers. One of the engineers that I counseled had a difficult time creating his "Here I Am!" Speech. Finally, I led him outside and pointed to an old tree across the street. "Tell me about that tree's life."

He replied that it must have been struck by lightning because there were some scars on its trunk. I said, "That's true. What else?" He said, "The power company cut a V through its upper branches." I replied, "True. What else?" He said, "I don't know." My response? "That tree obviously experienced some tough times, just like you. Yet, it is still standing tall and proud. <pause> Now tell me your "Here I Am! Speech"

"When I was a kid, my dad was an air traffic controller and private pilot. He had his own plane. Every weekend, we would go up in the plane. My dad put me in his lap as he flew the plane, and I pretended to be the pilot. When I was older, I set a goal to get my pilot's license at the same time I passed my driver's license. When I was 16 years old,

I earned both. When I graduated from high school, I went into the Air Force and began working on avionics equipment as a tech. Eventually, the Air Force promoted me to an avionics engineer. After I left the Air Force, I became an avionics engineer for (avionics company). As a matter of fact, if you are a (major airline) pilot flying a 767-400, I created the menu for the flat-panel display and determined when objects appeared in that display—so you are flying a plane with the menu I created. As the result of 9/11, (avionics company) had to lay off 300 people and I was one of them. Now I would like to go to work for another avionics company where I can help make flying safer for the pilots and the people they fly."

Do you feel the passion in his "Here I Am!" speech? Two weeks after he created his differentiator, he had an offer from another avionics company. That is how important your "Here I Am!" speech is. It needs to be sincere and passionate about what you have done and desire to do. Include a major accomplishment in your discussion. It is the beginning of your brand. It needs to be memorable for the person hearing it. They don't need to be able to repeat it. They need to remember it. Why? Many times, when managers are actively interviewing many candidates, they forget names and details; however, they remember stories. *I have repeatedly heard managers say, "I don't remember his name. They were the one that told the story about..."* Suddenly the other managers chime in and one of them remembers the name.

It's time for the bookmark again. Focus on your "Here I Am!" speech. Start to develop it. This usually is a task that takes a couple of days to hone. Remember, it must come from your heart. Trying to memorize it will fail because **you can't memorize passion, you feel it**. You know you have it when you can give it to a friend with total confidence and feel the passion in your branding.

Now that you are differentiating yourself and developing a brand for yourself, it is important to keep your brand consistent. It may evolve, and probably will as you interview and learn more about the requirements of the managers and companies where you are interviewing. Your "Here I Am!" speech and LinkedIn profiles need to be similar. Include aspects of your "Here I Am!" speech in your LinkedIn profile. As a professional recruiter, I look at the LinkedIn profiles of my candidates. Why? I simply want to learn more about them. Do they have a brand as a professional (*I am RecruiterGuy*)? Is it consistent with what they told me? Does their experience match the experience on their profile? Have they written short articles about the topic they say is their passion (looking for further proof of "passion")?

This is how a networking call may unfold. We will start with a "Warm Referral". Someone introduced you to the person you are calling.

"Hello Mary? When I spoke to John yesterday, he suggested that I should chat with you. Is this a good time to spend about 15 minutes?" (If yes, begin your "Here I Am! Speech.)

If it is not a good time to chat, ask, "When is the best time for me to call? If you prefer, I am available this evening at either 6 PM or 7 PM." (give them a choice, not a yes or no response). When you call them back, ask if this is still a good time to chat? If so, begin your Here I Am! speech.

Then ask, *"Who would you suggest that I speak with next?"*

What is your most valuable commodity during a job search? Networking names and phone numbers. Try to get 4 names and numbers on every call. That represents one day of networking contacts.

It's time for your progress review:

- ✓ By now, you recognize that you are involved in a sales process and as a result have completed your skills assessment with examples that demonstrate success with those skills and attributes.

- ✓ You have written at least 226 names on your list of warm contacts (family, friends and acquaintances). You are working on the other 150 to 250 names (good that you are exceeding expectations!). How about former professors? Doctors? People you met at the health club or during social events? Your list will grow continuously as you network.

- ✓ You have listed your accomplishments, beginning with the most recent and working backward.

- ✓ You have developed your "Here I Am!" speech. Practice it with people you know well first. It can be as simple as "Hey, I am working on a differentiator for my candidacy. Would you mind listening to it as I practice?" Most people would love to help you.

✓ Now you are developing your brand as a candidate. Our next step is to tie everything together in your resume. The combination of resume, LinkedIn profile and "Here I Am!" speech are your primary marketing preparations for networking and then interviewing.

It is time to get started on your primary marketing piece—your resume!

We Got This!

RecruiterGuy.com Series

STEP 4

Developing Your Marketing Piece—Your Resume

For every mile between New York and Los Angeles, there's a book published about resume writing. You may have already noticed on Amazon.com or BN.com. Some were written by people who are writers. Some were written by people who saw a chance to use some common sense and make some money. Others were written by professionals in the career development and human resource business. Obviously, in a book discussing the entire job-search process, I (in the recruitment business since 1981) cannot go into the detail a book on resumes alone would give; however, we can go over the basics to help you get back to work. Over the years, I have read more than 400,000 resumes and have seen some resumes that are truly classics. You'll hear about some of them in this step.

Before we get started, take a moment and watch this news clip. This interview was with Vinnie Politan on his CNN Headline News Show *Making It In America*. We discussed the Top 3 Resume Tips—https://www.youtube.com/watch?v=5g46MiCVOnU They are still my top three.

Occasionally, a candidate wants to demonstrate his creativity. When word processing first became popular, one candidate decided to create a box around his name and contact information. Unfortunately, he created a shaded box that covered the information. He didn't even look at it before sending it out! I did not call, but I imagined my call to his company: "Hey, who is the programmer at your company who used to work at ABCD Company?"

One of the most important fundamentals to understand is that the recruiting process is a sales process. Would you put up a billboard with the name of the company hidden? Doubtful. If your resume is unclear, your product—you—is difficult to sell.

We discussed this concept in the previous step and I will repeat it again in future steps. In the RecruiterGuy presentations on the recruitment process from both Job Search and Recruiting points of view, I subtitle the presentation, "Recruiting is Sales."

If the recruitment process is a sales process, then your resume is your marketing piece. As such, you need to include your accomplishments, especially for the past five years. This is not the time to worry about "bragging," as some candidates have said to me during career counseling. These are your accomplishments with the data and anecdotes to support your assertions. The resume also serves as the discussion jumping-off point during your interview. Resumes stimulate questions like this: "Tell me about your experience when you doubled the company's sales. Was that all a result of your efforts, or did other team members affect your results?"

Remember in the first step, I recommended you list the skills and experience that you do well and enjoy performing? Then I recommended that you build a story to demonstrate those specific skills? Now is the time to tell the recruiter the story you built around that achievement on your resume. Make sure you've formulated your story around your resume.

If your accomplishments are not on your resume, they may not be discussed in your interview and that's the point of the interview! Managers untrained in interviewing may not know how to draw the accomplishments out of you. Nor is it their job. YOU are selling, and they are buying.

Sell your strengths. Put your accomplishments on your resume.

Understanding that your resume is your marketing piece will possibly cause consternation for people who just discovered they are in a sales process. Visualizing yourself "on sale" can cause some discomfort. Don't worry; it's a universal process. This is the time to get your creative (honest) juices flowing. If you are in marketing, you may go much further with an imaginative presentation of your resume, possibly even on a video. Ensure all information is perfectly clear! Most positions require a more conventional approach.

So, you sweat all day writing the perfect resume. How much time will an experienced professional recruiter spend on it?

When I was on a recruitment consulting assignment with MCI Telecommunications, I hired a junior recruiter to assist me. The goal was to teach Andrea how to recruit. When I returned from each two-week interviewing trip, Andrea would bring a stack of resumes to my office to review before screening for our next trip. Because this was prior to e-mail and job boards, she generally brought me nearly 100 mailed or faxed resumes. One Monday, Andrea sat at a desk behind me while I read and separated the resumes into three stacks—definitely interested, definitely not interested, and the (painful) take another look.

When I was finished, Andrea told me that she had timed me as I read those resumes. Since I was from the East Coast, my knee jerk response was, "Didn't you have enough work for today?" Andrea was the best person I ever hired. Sometimes she had the ESP of Radar O'Reilly from "M.A.S.H." She replied that because I was teaching her how to become a recruiter, she needed to know how much time to spend reading a resume. If she timed the attention I gave each resume, she would have a sense for how much time to spend. Then she asked me what grabbed my attention. I told her that I would tell her, but first I wanted to know what she discovered.

She informed me that I spent as little as two seconds on some resumes, and those went into the "definitely interested" and "definitely not interested" stacks. I spent as much as 12 seconds on other resumes. Those went into the "definitely not interested" and the "take another look" stacks. She said I averaged six seconds per resume.

You have two to twelve seconds to get the attention of a professional recruiter. What are we looking for?

When we are conducting searches, we know specifically what experience our clients require. In a very quick scan, we can determine if that experience is on the resume. As we scan for that experience, we are making mental notes on the impact that person has made on his or her jobs. If your resume was not tailored for the position, we are not mind readers, and your resume may go into the "wrong" stack. You need to include the information needed to determine not only that you can DO the job. You need to Demonstrate that you can make impacts in that position based on your previous experience.

The convention in resume writing is to write your resume in the third person, as if someone were writing about you, and drop the pronouns. No "I" and "me." You also write your resume in past tense, even the responsibilities you have in your current position. This is a good time to review the list of action verbs in Appendix A. Where can you insert a stronger impact verb in each line of your resume?

Everyone who counsels candidates on resume writing has their own prejudices on the format. **These are the essentials: Keep it simple and easy to read.** If you are successful here, you are more likely to attract the attention of a recruiter or hiring manager. After all, what do they typically look for in an "impact performer?" Excellent communication skills and the positive, measurable impacts you have made.

I have another important rule: **Keep your contact information in a plain, easy-to-read format at the top of your resume in the BODY of the page, not in a Header. None of that fancy stuff like panels/boxes, bullet points/hyphens between addresses and phone numbers.** Also ensure that your contact information is in the body of the page, not the header. Why? Today most companies, including RecruiterGuy, stores your resume in an applicant-tracking system. The optical character reading (OCR) software may not be able to understand the fancy stuff (or read your header); and your resume will go into the manual loading process. That means it may never get into the system. If it does not get into the system directly, no one will read it, you will never be interviewed, and you will never know why.

Several times a year I receive resumes with no name or contact information. While I agree the information on your resume is important, being able to contact you is also bit of a priority. Your resume checklist needs to include a check to see if your name and contact information are easily found.

Today's world has changed one convention in your contact information on your resume. Today, you may include you town/city but not include your street address.

This an example of how your contact information may look:

John Doe
Park City, UT 84060
Home: (435) 555-0235 Cell: (801) 555-1593
jdoe@gmail.com

There are essentially two kinds of resume document formats. Most people are familiar with the **chronological format** where you list your most recent experience and work back in time chronologically. The other format is the **functional format** where you group your accomplishments together and then simply list your most recent employers in backward order, including dates of employment.

The advantage of the **chronological format** is that recruiters and hiring managers have a better understanding of your responsibilities in each position and when you made impacts on your employer's business. The potential disadvantage of the chronological resume is that short-term jobs tend to stand out more. If all your true impacts are in the past, say six years ago, managers wonder what you have been doing more recently. Try to list accomplishments in your current or most recent position.

The advantage of the **functional format** is the hope that recruiters and managers focus on your accomplishments and not on shorter tenures or the fact that accomplishments were made some time in your past. The disadvantage of the functional format is that most professional recruiters know what to look for or ask when they see a functional resume. In my experience, the other major disadvantage is that many managers feel a candidate is trying to cover something up if they see a functional resume.

Which format is my preference? Based on my experience working with thousands of hiring managers over 36-plus years, I prefer the chronological resume. This way I can see what accomplishments were made—and when. Bill, if you don't share these with your recruiter, who can you share it with? Do you strategize with your clients about their short-term jobs?

I like to see your name and contact information centered at the top of your resume (bold is nice). Look at the example above. Then I like to see **Summary:** (bold) justified on the left margin. In your summary, list headlines of some of your important accomplishments—it would look something like this:

> **Summary:** Saved company $150,000 by restructuring procurement process. Or, Consistently sold 125 percent of quota in past five years.

You may add more details on your summary accomplishments in the body of your resume in the Professional Experience area.

If you graduated from college, **Education:** (bold) would be next, after job experiences and impacts, also justified on the left margin. List your most recent degree first. Then follow below with other degrees (if you earned them) in reverse order—most recent first. The reason that I prefer Education next is that many people in large companies who retrieve resumes have a checklist, and a college education many times is one of those checks. One of the metrics recruiters are measured on is the number of "qualified resumes" they forward to the corporate recruiter. If they are in a time crunch, your resume may not make the cut. If education is at the bottom of your resume, the recruiter may miss it or worse, forget to check your professional impacts while searching for education.

Here is a HUGE caution: Degrees are the easiest information to verify on a resume. If you did not get the last two PE credits, the college/university still requires you earn them before you earn your degree. If you lie about your degree and are caught—and most likely today you will be caught—your employment offer will be rescinded, or you will be fired. That's not something that you will want to discuss in your next interview.

Several years ago, a candidate that I introduced to a company showed a college degree from a major university. When I checked his credentials, I discovered he attended the school but did not graduate. He was one class short of earning a degree. Over the years no one questioned him. Now we were interviewing him for a sales job for which he was eminently qualified (and that did not require a degree). When we discovered his deceit, I asked him why he lied about his degree. He responded that he thought he was "close enough." It cost him a job that he really wanted with a quality company.

This is a good time to talk briefly about honesty and resumes—and tell another story. There are two kinds of dishonesty and both have negative effects on your job search. The first is intentionally omitting skills (known as impacts or accomplishments) that you enjoy doing and in which you have a great track record. This is a lie of omission. While there may be times that you want to leave off a degree earned (it does not apply to the position), Don't leave out impacts.

Omissions have potentially negative impacts as well; it's a more important challenge to discuss. Think of yourself as the manager reading your resume. How would you feel if your candidate was imprecise, or worse, careless? It is very important that your resume paints an accurate picture of you as a professional. Not only does the complete resume establish trust with a potential employer, it increases your chance of getting the job.

Companies feel resumes and applications are legal documents that represent your background, and as such, need to be truthful. For instance, you may have had a job for a short time and for one or more reasons, it may not have worked out. Never let anyone suggest that you cover that job by stretching the end date of one job and the beginning date of the following job, effectively eliminating that experience from your resume. That's a lie. Don't leave it out completely; that's a lie of omission. Include the job. Then add the reason you left. Sometimes, companies paint an inaccurate picture of the job and responsibilities, just to get someone onboard. Other times the candidate accepted that job, then was offered a position that payed much more. Therefore, they resigned prior to their company spending a lot of money training them. Prepare yourself to describe exactly what happened.

Check out this television interview titled, "Liar, Liar Will Get You Fired" where we discussed the various ways I have seen people lie on their resume—and the potential ramifications. (Video goes away for a short period near the beginning)—https://www.youtube.com/watch?v=0XBCodWrirY

Some years ago, I was working with a candidate who was in IT. An honest, hard-working person, he was introduced to a major corporation who had hired me to conduct a search. They interviewed him and liked him so much, they extended him a contingent offer on the spot. The offer would become official upon successful completion of a background check and drug test (both normal today).

He took the drug test and within a couple of days, the results came back and he passed. He turned in his resignation notice and was prepared to start with his new company in two weeks. On the Friday before his Monday start, his offer was rescinded. He would not be allowed to start with the company. When I asked what happened, they told me he covered up his employment at one firm by extending his end date at one company and start date at the next. When I called him, he said his resume writer suggested the change before I interviewed him—that way he would not have to discuss the short tenure.

The client told me they probably would have hired him anyway, even if they had known about the short stint a one job. Their feeling was that if he would "lie" about something as small as this, what would happen if they had a major issue? Great point! That is the basis of behavioral interviewing. The candidate was distraught because he lost the opportunity to work at a truly great company and he now had no job. His previous employer had already hired his replacement.

Employment applications typically have verbiage that states you could be fired at any time (even years later) if you misrepresent your experience. It is important that your resume and application experience match.

Tell the truth on your resume.

Then write, **Professional Experience:** (bold) justified on left column. Below Professional Experience, write the name of your current/last employer (bold/left justified) and your dates of employment (bold/right justified). Below your employer's name, write your title (bold/left justified), followed by your most recent position. Then work backward. Here's an example of how that might look:

PROFESSIONAL EXPERIENCE:

IBM **May 2007 to Present**

Director, Consulting Services
Responsible for the growth of this Washington, D.C., division of Government Services

Consulting. Managed 200 consultants in the government services arena. Grew the division revenues by 65 percent in three years through hard work and client service. Recruited key consultants for contracts with the Department of Agriculture and the Department of Transportation.

- Secured contracts with government agencies where there was no previous contract with IBM.
- Grew the division profits 10 percent per year.
- Maintained high level of retention among consultants—85 percent.

If you have worked with the same company for a long time and held several positions within the company, write the name of your employer (bold/left justified) and your total dates of employment (bold/right justified). Skip a line and write your current/last title (bold/left justified) and your dates in that position (bold/tab right).

Employee 5.0

Here's an example:

PROFESSIONAL EXPERIENCE:

IBM   **May 2003 to Present**
Director, Consulting Services
August 2007 to Present

Responsible for the growth of this Washington, D.C., division of Government Services

Consulting. Managed 200 consultants in the government services arena. Grew the division revenues by 65 percent in 3 years through hard work and client service. Recruited key consultants for contracts with the Department of Agriculture and the Department of Transportation.

- Secured contracts with government agencies where there was no previous contract with IBM.

- Grew the division profits 10 percent per year.

- Maintained high level of retention among consultants—85 percent.

Senior Manager, Consulting Services
May 2003 to August 2007

Managed 100 consultants working on a project for the Department of Agriculture. Responsible for client contact and client service. Negotiated a new contract to measure IT efficiencies within the Department of Agriculture's Animal and Plant Health Inspection Service.

- Grew profits for these projects by 40 percent over three years.

Understand that your information in the body of the resume describing responsibilities is not in bold. When writing a resume, always begin sentences with an action verb in the simple past tense.

Never begin a sentence with "Have developed." Begin the sentence "Developed."

Write your resume with your responsibilities in paragraph format and accomplishments listed with bullet points. Some books recommend that you bullet point all your activities. Based on my experience, you should only list a few important accomplishments with bullet points for each position. Otherwise, in a resume with too many bullet points, your primary accomplishments may be overlooked. Remember, your resume is a marketing piece; you want to direct focus to your biggest accomplishments.

This is very important! **Do not put any personal information in your resume!** Like it or not, people use all the information you give them to decide whether you are a fit for their position or not. While companies cannot legally ask you for personal information, if you volunteer the information either on a resume or during an interview, they can use it.

An example I have used in my speeches is this. John Doe is an avionics engineer for Honeywell. He is interested in a position with Rockwell Collins in Cedar Rapids, Iowa. Jane Doe is an avionics engineer for Northrop Grumman and is interested in the same position at Rockwell Collins. When you look at their resumes, they have almost the same background in education and work experience.

John Doe goes sky diving a couple of times a year and listed that activity on his resume. Jane was advised not to list personal activities on her resume; therefore, she did not mention that she was the president of the sky diving club in Utah and goes out virtually every spring, summer and fall weekend to sky dive.

Both were called to interview with Rockwell Collins. The manager was surprised how close a call it was. Then she noticed that John Doe mentioned on his resume that he was a sky diver. She decided to hire Jane Doe because this was an important hire; and she didn't want to lose a key employee to a sky-diving accident. It was only after Jane started that the manager heard that she was a true sky-diving enthusiast.

That is the reason you need to avoid including skydiving, mountain biking, whitewater rafting and other "dangerous" outside activities on your resume for professional positions. On the other hand, include them if you are applying for a position with an outfitter or a company that supplies that type of equipment. The recruiting and interviewing process is a discrimination process. The hiring manager is trying to determine who is the best qualified and the best fit. The hope is that the discrimination is legal. It's simply best to avoid putting any personal information on your resume.

You can add your work in associations or voluntary organizations, particularly if you were a leader. If you are interviewing in a manager's office and see a service club plaque, it is okay to ask about their relationship with that club. If you belong to the same club but a different step, you have formed the basis of a relationship.

Once you finish your resume, read it aloud word by word. Then read it again backward aloud. Read it a third time forward aloud. Be aware that "form" and "from" both make it successfully through spell check.

I see "manger" substituted for "manager" almost monthly.

The same is true for "mange/manage," and their meanings are very different. There are many other words that match up that way—fan/fun/fin, chick/chuck, at/it/as/is, bite/kite, meet/meat, hear/here, peer/pear, peek/peak, etc. Use the "Find/Replace" function in your word processing program to check for these and other common mix-ups. Once you are totally satisfied it is perfect, ask someone who did not help you write your resume to edit it for you.

Remember spell check? One candidate wrote in a cover letter that he was a "detale-oriented professional" (does that hurt?).

Even universities are not immune to these mistakes. In August 2017, I saw a posting on LinkedIn where a university posted the need for a "Manger". I posted the following question, "Does this position come with or without straw?"

Therefore, it is critical to read your resume as an editor or ask someone to edit it for you. Only then is it almost safe to give to a company—just read it aloud one more time. Remember, your resume is your representation of you; you are selling your skills and talents. If it is written carelessly, this reflects your work.

In the spring of 1994, I was asked to present the recruitment process to 16 visiting Russian business people. They were from oil companies in southern Russia. Prior to the Soviet Union splitting apart, a central bureau matched candidates with companies. Candidates had no interviews, no tour, no decision. When they told you to report to that company, that's where you worked. The companies were on the other side of the coin. There was no interviewing process. They took the person the central bureau sent. They did not need to attract candidates. There were no recruiters. They picked up the phone and called the bureau—and people reported on Monday.

After the U.S.S.R became Russia again, those companies now needed to learn to compete for candidates and how to select the best candidates. That's why they were in northern Virginia that day. I spoke to them through a translator:

When we discussed resumes, I told the business people that a resume should be the perfect reflection of a candidate's work. If there is a typo in their resume, I... (with that I scrunched up a piece of paper and used a hook shot to toss it into the trash can). It was fun to watch their eyes follow the ball of paper into the trashcan, then glance back quickly at the translator who translated what I said. Then they laughed.

Your resume is the representation of your best work when you are trying to make one of the most important sales of your life—your ability to make impacts with a new company.

Another candidate wrote in a cover letter that he "would be a good fit for MCI" (my client). Then he wrote that companies such as Boeing (instead of MCI) need professionals who understood marketing—and then proceeded to use two more company names in place of MCI. I can't imagine that he was successful attracting an interview with that letter!

When you write a resume, it is best to understand that it is really a base for future resumes. Before you apply to a company, change words in your resume to reflect the verbiage in the company's job description. For instance, perhaps in your resume you were called a buyer at your last company. When you read the job description, it was almost a perfect match for your "buyer" position but their title is "purchasing agent." Then they used "purchased" instead of "bought." Change your words to match their words.

Save your new resume with the name of the company and date. Save each resume version moving forward. Leave a paper trail for yourself to build on in the future. You can track what worked and what didn't in the past. Always make changes and updates that list the same work but use different descriptive action verbs (simple past), nouns and adjectives.

Why go through this effort? Recruiters tend to take keywords from their job descriptions and job postings to search the resume database in their applicant tracking system (ATS). If they choose "purchased" as one of their key words and you wrote "bought," chances are pretty good that your resume will not be selected; therefore, it is best to make those changes before forwarding your resume.

Think of the applicant tracking system as a Labrador Retriever. When the recruiter types in a few keywords, it is like showing the rawhide bone to the dog. Then they click "search" in the ATS. The computer gets all excited just like a dog, and when it returns in a couple of seconds (not like the dog…), it shows its excitement by saying in the results that it is 90 percent sure this person is a good match. Its determination that a candidate is a good match comes from seeing the search words (keywords) multiple times in your resume.

Therefore, if you are replying on an Internet posting, save another copy of your resume under the "company's name and keywords". At the bottom of that resume, type "Keywords:" and then list all potential keywords from their job description where you have that experience. Raise the hits on the ATS system by demonstrating you have the right experience for the job. That's why applicant tracking systems will not replace humans in the search process...soon. Anyone can point in words; humans judge their veracity.

Remember to put your name on each page of your resume. Since your name is on the first page, the best practice is to use the header for the following pages—page numbers justified left and your name justified on the right. Resume pages tend to separate on a hard-working manager's desk. Many times, I have watched managers shuffle papers while searching for page 2. Thank goodness, we deliver resumes via electricity and pixels. You don't lose page 2 if you read it online.

This a sample chronological resume:

John Doe
Park City, UT 84060
Home: (435) 555-0235 Cell: (801) 555-1593
jdoe@gmail.com

SUMMARY: Grew division revenues 65 percent over three years...Grew division profits incrementally...Secured new government contracts for IBM...Maintained 85 percent consultant retention rate.

EDUCATION: MBA, University of Iowa, 2013
BS, Business, University of Utah

PROFESSIONAL EXPERIENCE:

IBM **May 2004 to Present**
Director, Consulting Services
August 2007 to Present

Responsible for the growth of this Washington, D.C., division of Government Services Consulting. Managed 200 consultants in the government services arena. Grew the division revenues by 65 percent in three years through hard work and client service. Recruited key consultants for contracts with the Department of Agriculture and the Department of Transportation.

Secured contracts with government agencies where there was no previous contract with IBM.

Grew the division profits 10 percent per year.

Maintained high level of retention among consultants—85 percent.

Senior Manager, Consulting Services
May 2004 to August 2017

Managed 100 consultants working on projects for the Department of Agriculture. Responsible for client contact and client service. Negotiated a new contract to measure IT efficiencies within the Department of Agriculture's Animal and Plant Health Inspection Service.

Grew profits for these projects by 40 percent over three years.

Booz, Allen, Hamilton   May 1998 to April 2004
Consultant

Project Manager for government process improvement projects. Created the first template for a financial process improvement project at Commerce Department. Developed spreadsheets that highlighted waste.

Led a team responsible for the Census Bureau financial restructuring, saving taxpayers $50 million in the first year.

ASSOCIATIONS: Lean Enterprise Institute, presented at conference "Instituting Lean Process Improvement in Federal Agencies."

This is a sample functional resume:

John Doe
Park City, UT 84060
Home: (435) 555-0235 Cell: (801) 555-1593
jdoe@gmail.com

SUMMARY: Grew division revenues 65 percent over three years...Grew division profits incrementally...Secured new government contracts for IBM...Maintained 85 percent consultant retention rate.

EDUCATION: MBA, University of Iowa, 2013
BS, Business, University of Utah

SKILLS: Excellent Manager, Creative, Experienced Kaizen Event Leader, Budget-Oriented Leader.

IMPACTS: Led a team responsible for the Census Bureau financial restructuring, saving taxpayers $50 million in the first year.

Grew the division revenues by 65 percent in three years through hard work and client service.

Grew profits for these projects by 40 percent over three years.

Secured contracts with government agencies where there was no previous contract with IBM.

Grew the division profits 10 percent per year.

Maintained high level of retention among consultants—85 percent.

ASSOCIATIONS: Lean Enterprise Institute, presented at conference "Instituting Lean Process Improvement in Federal Agencies"

EXPERIENCE:

IBM
Director, Consulting Services May 2004 to Present

Booz, Allen, Hamilton
Consultant   May 1998 to April 2004

While obviously both resumes were created for these examples, you can see why experienced hiring managers like to see when impacts were made.

Every company has its own culture and focus.

In your research for prospective employers, go to every page on their web site and get a sense of their priorities. If they have community service pages, read them because it gives you a sense of their social responsibility. More important, you may volunteer at one or more of the charities they sponsor. That's the way you build your resume in addition to the work; you participate in the community of a company.

Developing an effective resume is important for creating an interesting interview. The candidates who work to create five interesting interviews are the ones who generally receive offers.

Take time now to create your resume. Remember, this is a process. To be successful, let's lay a good foundation and then move forward.

What is the role of cover letters? Most recruiters who have been in the business for a long time do not read cover letters. Unless I am trying to get a sense for a candidate's writing style, I do not read the cover letter either. There is no guarantee a candidate even wrote the cover letter. Many resume writers or career counselors either write the resume and letter or counsel the person what and how to convey information. If the company requires a cover letter, compose a succinct one. Cover the information required and request an interview: don't waste anyone's time. Or your own.

Where does Employee 5.0 fit into this step on resumes? This step is one of the differentiators for Employee 5.0. Where most people wait until they need an updated resume, the last day of each quarter, Employee 5.0's habit is to review theirs. If they need to add a new skill, experience or accomplishments, they update their resume now. They may even tweak their resume now to better fit a new direction in their career. This enables Employee 5.0 to be light on their feet to change career direction instantly when opportunity presents itself.

This step is so important that we have two checklists—the Resume Checklist and the Job Search Process Checklist.

Resume Checklist

- ✓ Is the information on your resume accurate? Honesty is the only policy.

- ✓ Is your name and contact information easily found in the body of your resume (not Header!)?

- ✓ Are your degree and graduation date accurate?

- ✓ Did you write your resume in third person, simple past tense?

- ✓ Did you drop the pronouns and begin your sentences with action verbs? (See Appendix A)

- ✓ Did you discuss your most-recent experience first followed chronologically by previous experience?

- ✓ Did you include all the measurable impacts on your resume?

- ✓ Have you read your resume aloud? Did you run spell check? Did you run "Find/Replace" for words like *mange, manger, from* and *form*?

- ✓ Has a friend or associate read your resume as an editor? Did they look at spelling and grammar?

- ✓ Have you saved your resume in your word processing software? Did you print it—just in case?

- ✓ If a cover letter is required, have you composed one that is succinct and covers all the information required by the company?

After you have completed this checklist, let's move to your job search checklist. Think of RecruiterGuy as your job search project manager as he sits on your shoulder.

Job Search PROCESS Checklist

Put a check mark next to the completed items on your list. Work to complete the unfinished ones. This process will help you find your next job. Your job now is to complete each task:

- ✓ Review your list of professional and personal skills to see if you can improve the impact verbs. Only use words that you use in normal conversation. It's very embarrassing to use the wrong verb.

- ✓ Review the examples of the situations that required your skills. After thinking about your examples over the last few days, are there better examples that you can use? Again, the format is to discuss your action in the situation; tell a story around the skill. Then discuss what happened because of your influence or direct action.

- ✓ **People remember stories, not lists.**

- ✓ Develop a list of your positive, measurable impacts over the past 10 years, with focus on the last five years. List them from the most recent impacts backward. Develop **The 4 W's—What was the challenge? What was your response? What was the result? What did you learn?**

✓ If you still have old annual reviews, read them for impacts that you may have forgotten. Create your stories around the most important.

✓ Review and add to your list of 350 names of family, friends and acquaintances, neighbors, former peers/managers in your last company and previous companies, high school and college alumni, pastor/rabbi/spiritual mentor, banker, attorney, real estate agents, professors, doctors, and acquaintances from the health club. Look up their contact information in your address book, the phone book or use Google or Bing to search for them on the Internet.

✓ Join LinkedIn and invite everyone you feel can help you—and who you can help somewhere. Remember, it is important to give. When people accept your invitation, go through their network, and see if there may be contacts you forgot to enter on your list.

- ✓ This action may help you remember additional people to add to your spreadsheet. Remember, people know other people—and LinkedIn is a great example of how it can work.

- ✓ You have developed your "Here I Am!" speech. Continue to practice it with people you know well first. Your request may be as simple as, "Hey, I am working on a differentiator for my candidacy. Would you mind listening to it as I practice?" Most people would love to help you.

Now you are developing your brand as a candidate. Your resume is completed. The combination of resume, LinkedIn profile, and "Here I Am!" speech are your primary marketing preparations for networking and then interviewing.

If you have not completed all these steps, **put your bookmark back in here** and finish these processes. Remember, these are the fundamentals that will help you find your next job. Skating only extends your job-search process.

Let's pause here for a second. As you have been preparing your search, have you considered starting your own business? If you have, many community colleges bring businesspeople in to conduct classes on entrepreneurship and start-ups. Additionally, you should contact the Small Business Administration to discuss the process. Read some of the countless great books on the subjects and find mentors amongst the many who successfully started and run a business.

Let's cover the proper mental attitude for your job search!

STEP 5

You Got This!

We've covered a lot of information in the past four steps! You have put so much of your preparation time into this effort, you no doubt long for tangible results to demonstrate YOUR time and effort.

Remember, the job search is a sales process that requires preparation. The most prepared candidates who have the required skills are the first hired. Every Step that you worked through to this point is an important Step—

1. Working through your grief.

2. Listed your skills and attributes.

3. Created stories that demonstrate your skills and attributes—and improve your stories.

4. Created your networking contact spreadsheet with at least 350 names.

5. Set your goal for the job you desire and when you want to be in that position.

6. Developed your Hear I Am! speech.

7. Developed your resume.

This is a lot of work that you accomplished. You have successfully prepared yourself to catapult your way through the last steps to find your job. Take a moment to celebrate your preparation! Okay! That's long enough!

You are a professional! Prepare as a professional. Your benefit will be the success to find a job you love with a great company within 90 days or so, depending on the balance of your efforts.

As an executive career transition coach, my experience has demonstrated that at this point, some people are beginning to experience some frustration. Part of the frustration is the nature of the process and part is the fact that many professionals are transaction motivated—if I do this, I receive that (money, recognition, promotions).

You Got This! We are so close!

Just as in athletics and the performing arts, much of this process requires a proper mental attitude and preparation. I realize you are tired of hearing attitude, attitude, attitude. At this point, you are still experiencing the grieving process. Therefore, your mind is telling you things that are not true. Watch for these voices; they are not true. Your value to a company is enormous; past lay-offs are the result of forces out of your control. With each successful step of this process, you'll find your power returning. You will take action for yourself—and that feels great!

In 2001, I was diagnosed with renal cell cancer on my kidney. It was miraculous that it was discovered when it was so very early. I give credit to my guardian angel.

My kidney surgery was December 21. After my surgery, the nurses had me up on my feet and walking within 5 hours. They told me I would be able to leave the hospital sooner if I walked now. The surgery was major, but I am coachable. Therefore, my pole with anesthesia and I took off down the hall with the goal of being out of the hospital on Christmas—remember challenging and yet attainable goals?

In the middle of the first night, those voices began chirping in my head. The voices were saying,

"Your cancer is worse than they told you. You will die soon. The doctors just want you to have a nice last Christmas." My wife was working in the hospital that night. I found her in another unit. She reassured me that the doctors were telling me the truth. I was discharged on Christmas Day. I am convinced the reason was, I visualized being home on Christmas. As you may have noticed, the doctors were telling the truth. Those darn voices were causing me concern—they weren't reality.

Your voices do the same to you in your job search. They may say that you will never find a job as good as the last one. Your voices may say it is useless to do this preparation—and for what reason? Your voices may question the time you put into the preparation, saying you are wasting your time, instead of "Looking for a job!" I know because I have heard those words from executives I coached.

This is a great time to discuss the power of visualization. Let's get your inner voices focusing on the positive.

Visualization is a force so powerful that many of us don't understand until we experience it. Our brains can accomplish our dreams—if we train and believe. Call it confidence, call it faith, call it assurance. Whatever you call it, when you are confident of success, most times you succeed.

How do you become confident? You practice—you visualize success. How many times? All your life, no matter what you face.

For almost 20 years, I coached 7th and 8th grade girls' basketball in Maryland and Iowa. One 8th grade team heard my mantra and believed it—"Free throws win games!" Every evening I would end practice by saying this, "Tonight, before you go to sleep, picture yourself at the free throw line. Look up at the scoreboard. We are down one point. You have 2 free throws. There are 2 seconds left on the clock. If you make both free throws, we win by one point. Picture the fans behind the basket waving their hands and screaming at you to miss your shot. Picture the referee holding the ball waiting for you to set. Once you are ready, picture the bounce pass as it comes into your hands. Feel your confidence as you dribble the ball a couple of times. Then with your knees bent, elevate to your tip toes as you release the basketball in a perfect arc to the basket. Wave to the basketball as you release it to give it a nice backspin. Picture 'all net' as the ball floats through the net and you score!

Does this actually work? You be the judge. With this one 8th grade girls' basketball team, our last tournament was a 3 game tournament. We won each game in sudden death overtime…with a good free throw. Free throws win games—and **Visualization Works!**

Picture yourself in your work environment, as best you can. Include every detail you can. If you are a project manager, visualize yourself building consensus with the team you are supporting. If you are a surgeon, visualize a perfect surgery. If you are teacher, visualize yourself engaging your class. Then, if you have a company you are targeting, picture yourself already working there, making positive, measurable impacts—and having fun (because that's important too!). Keep that vision in your mind. Picture it every evening and every morning. Give your brain something with a positive focus!

Now, let's get on with work at hand. Our next process is enjoyable if you give back to other people. You learn about them and their dreams, and possibly contribute to their success. Meanwhile, some of them may be instrumental in helping you in your search.

In the spirit of visualization, every morning when you are preparing for your day, and every evening before bed, stand in front of the mirror. Look at yourself and smile confidently. Then say aloud...

I Am A Professional!
I GOT THIS!

Visualization is a powerful tool. If you network faithfully, and practice visualization, you improve your chances of finding a job sooner. Is it worth trying? What do you have to lose? Once you find your new position, continue to practice visualization in your work and personal life.

YOU GOT THIS! Now let's Learn LinkedIn Literacy!

RecruiterGuy.com Series

STEP 6

LinkedIn Literacy

Let's talk about social networking. During the past couple of years, you have been bombarded with all kinds of social-networking opportunities—LinkedIn, Facebook, Twitter, YouTube, Instagram, etc. More are on the way. If you are not comfortable with iPhones, iPads, Android phones, Microsoft Surface pads, and other handheld computers that allow you to talk, check e-mail, and set appointments simultaneously, you probably are not very comfortable with the social-media tools. On the other hand, maybe you're more "OMG U text 4 hrs!"; and know these tools are simply arrows in your quiver.

Employee 5.0 is prepared to use these tools to propel their careers forward. LinkedIn is a tool that may even benefit them by identifying directors and executives in their own company. A contact is made with them. That executive sees that

Employee 5.0 is in their company already—easy recruit! All managers like easy hires!

Separate your social networking from your professional networking. If you connect with a company on Facebook, it can see your posts and pictures. Some may be embarrassing, or worse, disqualify you from a job.

The owner of a recruiting firm told me they introduced a candidate to a financial institution. The interview went very well, so well they extended a contingent offer to the candidate. The candidate accepted their offer. The company is very thorough when they vet their candidates. The client looked up the candidate on Facebook. The person enabled everyone to see his pages. Evidently some of his posts to friends were viewed to be unacceptable for this firm (evidently anarchists and financial institutions are poor matches...) and they rescinded the offer. Remember, everything that is public may be viewed and used in the final decision to determine if you are the best fit for a position. ***Like it or not, you are constantly being measured by someone.***

The current standard for professional social-media networking is LinkedIn.com. More than 460 million people worldwide have profiles on it as of 2017. Only one of those contacts is needed for you to find the perfect job.

Once you begin developing your brand as a candidate or employee, it's good to develop your profile on LinkedIn. Working on LinkedIn can take as much time as you want to dedicate to it. That is my caution to candidates and companies alike: Every networking/sourcing method costs something. Sometimes it's money; sometimes it is time. If it is time, it must be done well or you (or they) lose credibility with the audience. Remember to work on your LinkedIn profile during the time when you cannot network—early morning or in the evening—outside of Prime Networking Time.

Recruiters recognized early how powerful LinkedIn could be as a recruiting tool. What's better than a free list of names with their professional backgrounds? Everything is to like here! From a candidate's perspective, it's a strong networking tool because it can be a great way to introduce yourself to a company you like or to a new region where you want to move.

As you complete your profile, keep in mind that recruiters search for key words. They may be words that are in their job descriptions or they may simply be titles. In some industries/companies you may be a "buyer." In others, your title may be "purchasing agent." Ensure that both are in your profile. You may be a sales professional, account manager, account executive or two dozen other titles. What do you do professionally? You sell something to someone.

Your LinkedIn summary gives you an opportunity to discuss your brand and impacts over the past several years. If you have presented to groups and want to continue doing so, be sure to list at least some of your recent presentations. The information in your summary should give readers a sense of your proficiencies.

If you are someone who reads literature about your industry, write a 400 to 600-word review of the book you're reading. Click on "Write an article" on your LinkedIn Home page. Talk about your experience and how that book may affect others in the same area or industry. All the positive information you add to your LinkedIn profile gives other people a sense for who you are. It also adds professional credibility.

If you have a presentation that you feel would be valuable to share, you may add it to your profile. This is another way to demonstrate your knowledge within your field and develop the perception of expertise. A person's perception is their reality.

After I presented the webinar "Why the Best Qualified Candidate Rarely Gets the Job," I added the presentation to my LinkedIn profile; and received thanks and congratulations for the presentation. This is a way for me to provide potential clients a reason to have a conversation with me.

Remember that networking is a two-way street. Part of your cost of participation is to benefit the other people in your network. As you link with other people and grow your network, some people may have really impressed you with their actions when you worked with them. Write a sincere recommendation for them on LinkedIn that describes a situation or position where they were particularly effective, and mention the positive impacts of their actions. By the way, write the recommendation in a word-processing program to take advantage of spell check and double check to ensure you spelled their name correctly. They may decide to accept your recommendation. Some of those people will write a recommendation for you, but don't request it from them. The recommendations you receive will be shared for others to view on your profile page.

Join groups that are either in your field or in the field where you are seek employment. In the search box, write the professional field that interests you. Click on the search button. Profiles of people will show below another menu bar that includes "Groups". Click on "Groups" and you will find groups within that area of your interests.

Then click on "Join Now". Many groups are moderated. Therefore, the moderator will either accept you as a member or not. Unless you have a history of spamming groups, generally they will accept your request. Most of those groups post jobs within the group, so this is an excellent opportunity to see what other members are looking for. Additionally, members may ask public questions looking for responses from other members. This is an additional way for you to build on your brand and show that you are an expert in a professional area.

Once you begin joining groups, it is a good idea to return to them to read what's trending in that group. If you have positive comments based on your professional experience, add them. Your responses build your brand as a professional in that field. You find Groups on the top menu bar that does not change as you navigate LinkedIn. The last menu item looks like the side of a Rubik Cube with the word "Work" below. Click on either the side of the cube or on "Work". This is where you may view the Groups you joined.

Beware of your posts. Never post something that you would not want to read on the front page of the *New York Times* tomorrow. LinkedIn can provide you with a wonderful opportunity to blast someone or some company. Don't do it! You can understand how poorly that reflects on you as an expert in your field. In addition, what company wants to hire someone who disparages companies? What would that person do as an employee?

For instance, I responded to a question on whether age discrimination exists. It was interesting to read the posts of unemployed human resource folks; some of these responses were not professional. My attitude has always been if a company is silly enough to discriminate against me based on age, I really would not want to work with them. A couple of people commenting on the topic were just being a little too forthcoming about their feelings. I wrote them a personal note and asked them if they were the one looking for a human resource professional and saw their response, would they contact someone with that response? The next day both posts were removed.

In the top menu bar on your "home" page on your LinkedIn profile, click on "My Network". When you click on My Network, you will see how many professionals have linked directly with you. Click on "See All". You may sort on most recent additions first, first names, or last names. If you prefer, click in the search box to the right and search on your connection's name.

LinkedIn uses a fuzzy logic to suggest people that you may want to connect with on LinkedIn. All you need to do is click on a name and invite the person to join your LinkedIn network (Click on "add to your network.") I prefer to write my own succinct invitation instead of the stock invitation provided by LinkedIn. **A personal request to link is more likely to be accepted than a stock invitation. As you read their profile, what have they done professionally or personally that matches your interests? Briefly add that to your invitation. Did you graduate from the same schools? Give them a reason to connect.**

Would you like to source more potential contacts through your current contacts? I call this method "Data Mining." Of course, true Data Miners may not call this process. But this is an effective way to quickly grow your LinkedIn network within a certain field.

Click on a person's name who is connected to you on LinkedIn. When you look at their profile page, look at the right column. Do you see the titanium laying there for your taking?? Above the column, the title reads, "People Also Viewed". Many of these people have similar backgrounds or industries. This is a very powerful way to grow your network quickly. Remember to send them a personal invitation based on their profile. When you go to their profile, look at their "People Also Viewed" column. Generally, there are even more people there for you to link!! Eureka! This is a titanium mine! Work the mine. Invite and don't worry about their location. They are linked to everyone across the US and the world—probably someone in your town.

In June 2013, my client paid me to spend one afternoon to develop a list of as many Agile IT Consultants in New York City as I could find. It sounded like a great challenge. My tool of choice was LinkedIn. My process was to first find an Agile IT Consultant that was linked directly with me. Then I began to drill down using "People Also Viewed." I invited the consultants whose profiles resonated with me—and maybe because they had many connections too. During the afternoon, those consultants began to accept my invitations. When I had a large pool, I focused on those Agile IT Consultants in the New York City area. In 5 hours, I listed 80 Agile IT Consultants in the New York City area with the name of their company. The consultants who were linked directly with me included emails and sometimes phone numbers. Think like a detective or a researcher—"what would happen if I...?"

As you are creating your LinkedIn profile, people will begin to discover you and ask you to join their LinkedIn network. Welcome the invitations that make sense. LinkedIn coaches you only to accept or invite the people you know well; however, I accept other people that appear to have legitimate, appropriate job histories that match my interests. I do not accept everyone.

In the latest iteration of LinkedIn, you see how many people have viewed your profile recently. Initially you are reaching out, not driving people to you. With articles and participation in LinkedIn, your professional branding will drive people to your profile. This is the reason that grammar and spelling must be perfect. Your profile is your brand as a candidate and as a professional in your field. Work towards growing your LinkedIn connections to 501 plus connections. Focus on connections nationwide in your field, industry, interests. Widen to professionals in your town and state. Then add additional connections from your College programs.

Beware of the time you spend in social media. Social media can be very seductive and addictive. Always aim for balance while networking. Your most productive time needs to be spent on the phone or in person.

While I was a young recruiter, a friend always referred to the prime candidate contact time as "Prime Time." Use Prime Time to do your

phone and personal networking. Set aside social media for your non-Prime Time work, such as early mornings or evenings.

Job Search PROCESS Checklist —

- ✓ Let's go to the beginning. Where do you feel you are relative to the stages of grief? Why do I keep bringing this up? I want you to be aware of your feelings—and know this is normal. Now add visualization of acceptance to your feelings.

- ✓ **Employee 5.0**—use LinkedIn to continue to grow your network. Make a habit to invite important network additions every weekend—non-Prime Time. Remember, they may take a month or so to accept.

- ✓ How many people are listed in your Networking spreadsheet? It is important to get your number up to 350 names and contact numbers. Remember, you just need to know the name of the company. Look up their general phone number—old school sourcing!

- ✓ Are you still adding skills and attributes to your lists? You should occasionally remember something that you forgot. Remember to add them, asterisk the ones that you enjoy, and build a story around the frame—**The 4 W's**—What was the challenge? What was your response? What was the result? What did you learn? You will need this for your interviews!

- ✓ Take time to review your LinkedIn Profile. Ensure it reflects your brand. Add articles and professional book reviews of 400 to 600 words to build the perception of you as a professional.

- ✓ Are you actively building your LinkedIn connections? The more direct connections, the more people you may network successfully. Feel free to request a link with me. https://www.linkedin.com/in/RecruiterGuy/ I have over 4,800 direct connections.

- ✓ Check your LinkedIn privacy to ensure your connections may see professionals in your network. Otherwise, they may check after they accept your invitation and then remove you. That is my practice. You may select your privacy by clicking your photo in the top menu bar.

- ✓ Tonight—and every night—stand in front of the mirror. Look at yourself confidently, smile and say aloud:

I Am A Professional!

I GOT THIS!

Now, let's move forward towards making great strides in networking to a new position by sourcing prior to networking!

STEP 7

Sourcing Prior to Networking

When I coach executives and other professionals who recently left their positions, they are visibly in shock. As we discuss how to find new positions, many have no clue how to source positions. They were always recruited by someone who knew their skills and contributions (networking). Suddenly, they need to figure out how to find work.

A key attitude is to assume the role of a Detective. "What if I look here? What happens when I click there?" This is how professional recruiters source companies where they sell candidates. In today's world, little is cut in stone. In the past, professionals would go to the *Wall Street Journal* back pages to seek new positions or possibly ask a recruiter who has built a relationship with them.

What tools are available today? The Internet provides us with many ways to research companies. Are all positions posted on the Internet? No. Generally, executive positions for larger companies are not posted. Those companies either have someone in mind or are willing to pay a retained recruiter fee.

There are many possible reasons why companies do not post those positions. Here are a few:

1. There is an incumbent and they do not want that person to hear the company seeks to replace them. For the recruiter, this is the definition of a "confidential search." You may have either been the beneficiary of such a search; or, possibly the victim of one.

2. The company has a succession plan in place and knows who they will promote.

3. Some companies do not have the internal talent to source and screen high level professional candidates.

4. Companies may not want to be involved in directly sourcing candidates from other companies; and prefer some plausible deniability. They don't want other companies

to learn that they are poaching. I tell my client they may reply that they told their contract recruiter to stay away from that company—Bad RecruiterGuy!

Employee 5.0—this is how you work your way to one of these hidden positions. Network your way to the influencers prior to their opening!

How do you find those positions and interview for it? Unless you are on that specific recruiter's radar, probably not through them. Proven time and again, the best way to interview for professional positions is to network your way in.

You know who your current—or most recent—company's competition is. That is a start. Many positions are the same across many companies—Accounting, Finance, Marketing, Customer Service, IT, Human Resources, etc. How important is industry specific experience in each of those fields? Let's say it is nice but not required.

Over the years when clients told me that the candidate MUST have this industry experience, I asked why this specific industry? Occasionally, the requirement was a specific degree.

In 1986, my contingent recruiting client was a defense contractor. They recently hired a programmer analyst through me who came from AMTRAK. They called me with another need for a programmer analyst. When we were discussing the requirements for a financial applications programmer analyst, the IT Manager told me the candidate must have 4 years of experience with financial/accounting systems and a degree in Finance, Computer Science, or Management Information Systems. By that time, I had been a contingent technical recruiter (headhunter, if you will) for 5 years.

Since this position was not a hard science or research position, I asked the manager if the person could have 6 years of financial/accounting applications experience and a degree in Math. He said, "No!" Then I asked if the candidate could have 7 years of financial/accounting applications experience and a degree in Music. The manager was getting upset and asked me what I did not understand about the degree requirement. "If the candidate does not have a degree in Finance, Computer Science, nor Management Information Systems, they are not qualified!"

What a wonderful coincidence occurred that morning! I came across his resume in our files and saw his degree. His question gave me an opening. My question seemed pretty simple since I was following his logic, "I was just looking at your resume this morning, and saw your degree was a BS.

Zoology from the University of Maryland. Does that mean you aren't qualified for your IT Manager position?" He asked me where I found his resume. I told him in our files. He asked me how we received it. I told him he must have mailed it to us (no email those days—yes, I am that old!). He hung up on me—guess he wasn't qualified for his job...

Therefore, I do understand that sometimes companies have unreasonable requirements. However, it is their company and they are legally allowed to have requirements that drive the best candidates away. Many times they are discriminating from a legal perspective.

Your attitude in those cases needs to be very simple—"I probably would not be happy there." Then move on. You have work to get done!

The same is true of age discrimination. Does age discrimination occur? Not legally, but of course it occurs. I have been a recruiter long enough to watch it bite some people in their late thirties claimed that people in their fifties would not understand the current market. Time flies by for all of us. Suddenly, they are in their fifties and out of work. They claim it is not fair! "The younger generation say we are too old to understand the new generation." Love it when Karma works! Please understand that the best action is to find someone in that company who has worked with you and knows how your skills will benefit that company. Then, he or she introduce you to a decision maker. If you are unable to network your way in, the only effective action is to simply move on. At this point, you do not need the negative energy from pounding your head against a wall.

Understand one fact. Most hiring managers have not been trained how to effectively interview and select the best qualified candidate. If that is the case, they will try to hire someone who looks like them from an age, experience, race, religion, and gender perspective. Therefore, they don't feel they are discriminating. They feel they are simply looking for candidates with their background, so they will also succeed. In my experience, these managers are not intentionally discriminating. They are acting on what they know—and that may be someone with their experience will help them succeed.

On the other hand, there are amazing CEO's who really understand the value of diversity. William McGowan, Founder and Chairman of MCI Telecommunications was one of those people. MCI Telecommunications was my first recruiting client in 1981—and remained one of my best clients until 1994. This was during the period when MCI demonstrated AT&T was acting as a monopoly. Eventually his company was key in the break-up of the AT&T monopoly.

McGowan would interview candidates for MCI. During his interview, he welcomed them to MCI and told them not to plan a long career there. "Join us for four or five years and contribute. Then leave and learn new things somewhere else and contribute there. After four or five years, return to MCI and make new contributions in a position with more responsibilities." I saw several people take McGowan up on his counsel.

When I worked at MCI on a thirty-month recruiting contract for IT professionals, we recruited people of all ages, races, gender, etc. It did not matter. What did matter was they had to perform—and most times they did perform because working there was fun at that time.

Let's get back to sourcing positions!

In addition to LinkedIn, where can you find companies who may need your services? There are more sources than you can count, especially with Google and Bing.

Let start with local sources. Have you looked at the membership of your local **Chamber of Commerce**? The local city/town **economic development**

organization? (They brag about the new companies they attracted to the area.) The **State Economic Development Agency**? (When we decided to leave Iowa, I met with the **Governor's Office of Economic Development** in Salt Lake City. They convinced me to bring my consulting business to Park City, UT.)

Have you gone to the library and read the local **business journals**? There is another resource in the Library Reference section—**MNI Manufacturers Directory**. They are printed by state and list every single manufacturer in the state, even as small as one employee. In the directory are the name of the company, address, what they manufacture, their revenues, and executives' names. It can be a powerful tool.

And you thought the library was old fashioned! Just spend a few minutes visiting with the Reference librarian, who may give you more leads! They may be lonely in today's world and are excited to help!

Of course, go online. Try these job boards to identify potential openings—just don't apply yet:

www.Indeed.com—now the largest job board

www.Monster.com—lost some of its shimmer but still a tool to be used.

www.CareerBuilder.com—falling further behind Indeed

www.Beyond.com—job board

List of 50 niche job boards (niche job boards focus on specific, and sometimes, narrow fields of work, i.e., accountants, nuclear plant engineers, banking, etc.)

https://www.smartrecruiters.com/blog/best-50-niche-job-boards/

The Financial Executive Networking Group **(www.thefeng.org)** learns about executive openings and shares them with its membership. This is primarily for CFO professionals, and is described as a niche group.

This is your research to find companies and openings. Create a spreadsheet that lists companies who are or have searched for people with your skills. Your spreadsheet should include a column for the company's website. Research their website. Then go to LinkedIn. In the search box on LinkedIn, type the company's name. Click on the company when the results come up. Then you will see the names of the people who work for the company on LinkedIn. Pick and choose who you want to link with on LinkedIn. Is this a great world—or what? Importantly, this is how you identify companies who do not yet know they need you!

Remember, in large companies, the most junior person in Human Resources is the person retrieving resumes from the applicant tracking system. Unless their system identifies you as a perfect fit, you will not be chosen—and your resume will remain in the black hole.

When professionals apply for positions online, many recruiters and career transition professionals call it "Posting and Praying." Why? Rarely are applicants contacted by the company. Even more rarely are they interviewed. What percentage of jobs in 2016 were filled through "Posting and Praying?" Somewhere between 8% and 10%. Not good odds.

The career transition industry has found that in strong employment economies and poor employment economies alike, the average is 74% to 76% of all positions are filled through networking—Now We Are Talking! When Human Resource Departments complain that metric is incorrect, they do not factor how many times someone networked with one of their employees. That employee told the candidate that the first action is to post for the position online. Then their networking contact asks the appropriate hiring manager to interview their networking contact. You may ask, why would they help me like that? They may simply want to help—and many times companies offer referral bonuses when the employee refers someone they hire. Win—Win!

Now that you know what percentage of positions are filled through networking, let's discuss the metrics the career transition industry discovered about professional job seeker activity.

If you talk/meet with 2 new people per week, it will take you a year to find a job.

If you talk/meet with 10 new people per week, it will take you 6 months to find a job. Sobering, huh?

If you talk/meet with 20 new people per week or 4 per day—2 in the morning and 2 in the afternoon, it will take you 90 days to find a job.

In my experience coaching executives, these numbers hold very true.

Several years ago, a senior account executive with a successful IBM career followed by a successful career with another company was laid off during a reorganization. (Remember what I said about companies not doing a good job measuring employees' worth?) This person knew how to sell!

She attended several of our May Park City Career Network meetings. Then she shared that she wanted to take the summer off to spend it with her children. Certainly understandable. At the end of August, she called and said she needed to get going on her search. We chatted about her required effort. She committed to finding a job in 90 days. This professional set about networking with at least 4 people per day. Almost to the 90 days later point, a top tier consulting organization hired her; and she is successfully selling on the enterprise level. She did it through networking persistently.

You can do it also! Now you know why you need at least 350 names. You will go through 80 contacts per month. The next step teaches you how to Effectively Network and keep building your list of contacts!

Job Search PROCESS Checklist—

- ✓ Let's go to the beginning. Where do you feel you are relative to the stages of grief? Why do I keep bringing this up? I want you to be aware of your feelings—and know this is normal. **Now add visualization of success finding the perfect job!**

✓ This is very important—How many people are listed in your Networking spreadsheet? This is the next step. It's important to get your number up to 350 names and contact numbers. Remember, you just need to know the name of the company. Look up their company's general phone number—old school sourcing!

✓ Are you still adding skills and attributes to your lists? You should occasionally remember something that you forgot. Remember to add them, asterisk the ones that you enjoy, and build a story around the frame—situation, your action, your result, and what you learned. You will need this for your interviews!

✓ Take time to review your LinkedIn Profile. Ensure it reflects your brand. Add articles and professional book reviews of 400 to 600 words to build the perception of you as a professional. While unemployed work to add one professional article per week. This is your job—build credibility and a following on LinkedIn.

✓ Are you actively building your LinkedIn connections? The more direct connections, the more people you may network successfully. Feel free to request a link with me. https://www.linkedin.com/in/RecruiterGuy/ I have over 4,800 direct connections. **You need to have at least 501 direct connections so people looking at your profile see you have 500+ connections!** Right or wrong, this is one-way recruiters measure a professional's credibility.

✓ Check your LinkedIn privacy to ensure your connections may see professionals in your network. Otherwise, they may check after they accept your invitation and then remove you. That is my practice. You may select your privacy by clicking your photo in the top menu bar.

- ✓ Tonight—and every night—stand in front of the mirror. Look at yourself confidently, smile and say aloud:

I Am A Professional!

I GOT THIS!

Now let's prepare to network!

STEP 8

Effective Networking To Your Next Position!

Are you tired of posting to the black holes on the Internet and company webpages job postings? You know them—tantalizing job titles and job postings where no one ever answers other than the automated thank-you, response.

Stand up and take control of your search! All too often, candidates try what they perceive is the easy route to find a job—simply getting on the Internet and posting their resume to dozens of companies at a time. Unfortunately, after all those postings, they never receive a call.

Then frustration sets in and they find themselves complaining that it's all a waste of time—and then they do it again tomorrow and the next day.

Please understand that Internet job postings are essentially automated newspaper ads. *The beauty of the Internet from a company perspective is that instead of having to handle each resume, the Internet response never needs to be handled by a human.* That line should give you something to think about. Now you know why you never receive a call.

You also know the metrics in networking present a very compelling argument why networking needs to be your **Prime Time activity**. You must network with 4 people per day to find a job in 90 days.

As a rookie recruiter, I was required to speak to 40 candidates per day. It was great training. I did not have the Internet in 1981. Heck, we did not have a computer! That came 5 years later. **You can talk with 4 people per day. You Got This!**

Some companies out there are excellent recruiting machines. But in my experience, most companies are trying to recruit the same way they always have, without really learning that recruiting is sales. They do not understand that the candidate experience is as important as the consumer experience, if not more important. A great employee is money in the bank. Chances are, most companies that do not understand the importance of the candidate experience are the same companies you have not heard from. Isn't it amazing that sometimes you do not hear from companies even after you told them in your inquiry that you are a happy client?

Recruiting is sales! When I speak at association and corporate meetings and webinars, I demonstrate how the sales process and recruiting process mirror each other perfectly.

I understand that you are tired of hearing about networking and how many jobs are filled by networking and networking breakfasts and networking on social media and networking on the phone and networking this and networking that. No one seems to want to slow down and truly describe networking. Everyone seems to be too busy networking to explain it.

Many times, job seekers complain that they do not know how to "network." This is the simple truth—everyone has networked since he or she was a child.

Do you remember a time when a brother, sister, or friend had something you wanted? Maybe it was a toy, a piece of candy, or free tickets to a movie. What did you ask them? "Where d'ya get THAT?" That is networking! We have been networking our entire life—And didn't even know it!

Networking can occur in every conversation you have. It is simply the exchange of ideas that can benefit one or both parties. Networking is not only used in job searches, it is successfully utilized in business and business development at all levels. It's also used constantly in life, from asking a new neighbor where the best grocery store is to approaching a policeman for directions. It's not some huge monster. The term just feels that way.

Networking is just one conversation at a time in person or over the phone. It's the consistent use of those interactions that benefit people. Networking conversations require focused listening skills. You need to be able to listen to your conversation, and sometimes, infer what this person needs. Then ask them if they tried this solution or another to solve their problem. Sometimes fresh eyes on a problem produce an AHA! Moment for the recipient. They may also be able to provide you with your AHA! moment with their solution for you or provide you with the best person to meet.

Now that you have a better sense of networking, it should become easier. Of course, those first few conversations may be tough to begin. Once you start seeing results from some of your networking, you will build confidence in your ability to contribute to these conversations. Remember when you were in a sport or practicing with a musical instrument or dealing with some code that was misbehaving, and your mentor replied, "Practice makes perfect!" You wanted to smack them, correct? Reflecting on your experience, will you admit it's true? Of course, it is!

As we work through this step, we will discuss how to practice networking so it becomes second nature for you.

You may never be a great fan of networking, but you will become more confident in your skills while working the process.

One very important concept of networking is that successful networking involves both *Give and Take*. The first step in successful *networking* is listening.

Focus on the person who is talking with you. Ask yourself, "How can I help them?" Ask them questions to clarify your thinking. Then try to make helpful suggestions for them.

While looking for a job, it is easy to be focused on your situation without thinking about the other person. After all, you do have bills to pay. Your cost to belong to the networking society is your ability to give back to the people you contact. Once you demonstrate that you will give suggestions to the other people with whom you network, they will take your call more enthusiastically and offer corresponding suggestions to you.

The law of nature is, "What you give is what you will receive." Be a giving person during this process. Being an active listener, a person who assimilates information and then creates a thoughtful response is generally in demand. Pay attention in every conversation. You never know when a small clue of an opportunity may emerge.

Be careful that you are not like an opera singer warming up—me, me, me, me!

Have you attended a Chamber of Commerce after hours or networking social where people become the opera singer warming up? They do not understand that instead of engaging their listeners, they are driving them away. Don't pitch to your new acquaintance! Listen. They have a story to tell—and their story may ultimately benefit you! Remember when we discussed the job search process as a sales process? In the sales process, it is best to talk in terms of the other person's interest.

What is the most effective way to network for a new position?

The first step is to develop your "Here I Am!" speech. This is also known as an elevator speech or one-minute commercial. It needs to come from your heart and give a quick snapshot of your background, your current situation and what you want to do next. It shouldn't be longer than 1 minute. You worked on your "Here I Am!" speech in Step 3, "What's Next? Here I Am!" I gave an example of an effective "Here I Am!" speech.

Once you are comfortable with what you will tell contacts, it is important to refer to your list of people to contact. I discussed this list creation in depth in Steps 1 and 3. Don't limit that list to those who know you well. Include any people who know who you are. Your list could include people from your former employer who know your strong work ethic, friends, neighbors, people from church, a store, or your bank. How about the parents of your children's friends? Include everyone. I understand that you are thinking we already discussed creating a list. Your list needs to be dynamic. We need to squeeze every single person from your brain. The one you skip, may be the one who wants to hire you. The more the better. During a job search, your most important commodity is names and phone numbers, particularly referred names and phone numbers. Develop a spreadsheet of everyone you know, including all acquaintances, with a phone number and information about where they work (if you know). Do you belong to a service organization like Rotary Club or Lion's Club? Do you belong to Toastmasters? This may be a good time to join some of those organizations. Remember, networking involves giving back to your community. We discussed why positive thinking and positive action generates positive results. This work needs to be performed, even if you are still swirling in the pool of grief. Remember the whitewater analogy? This is how you power your way out of the grieving process.

Employee 5.0 constantly works to stay visible during this process and while they are employed. Become active within service organizations that speak to your passions. It could be Rotary, Lions, Sierra Club, or any charity that speaks to your heart. The people you meet who match your passions may be able to help you find a company whose culture matches your heart.

Develop a second spreadsheet of companies you have targeted.

Once you have identified potential target companies, spend some time researching them. Comb through their web site. Where are the opportunities for you to help them? Try to understand their challenges. Who is their competition? Based on their web site, what challenges can you help them overcome? This information is important while networking and during an interview. During research, take copious notes—either cut and paste your notes on the company to a document or print pages of its web site. Once you have conducted research on their website, Google, Bing, and Glassdoor, look at the company on LinkedIn. Then click on their people. See who you are directly connected and who may be willing to link with you. You know how you learn best. During your research, you may discover the company is not a good fit for you. That's fine. It is as important for you to cross companies off your list as add them. Their competition may be the right company.

Knowledge is power!

When our daughter was looking at colleges, we spent a couple of days traveling and visiting several colleges and looking for the right fit for her. As we were driving home, she apologized that none of those colleges seemed like the right one. I told her not to apologize. "We now know three colleges are not a fit. Let's keep looking." Eventually, she walked onto a college campus and said, "This is the one!" It turned out to be a great fit for her, both personally and education-wise.

You are going through the same process right now. Some companies are added to your list. Others are crossed off. That is part of the process. Remember, you are trying to find that job that is so much fun you'll say, "Wow! I even get paid to do this!"

Finally, if you have a LinkedIn network, identify people you want to call and contact with there; some of these are your "cold calls." Use the LinkedIn network to meet people who may be instrumental to setting up an interview with you. We worked on developing your list over the last few steps. Your list gives you a track to run. This is how important networking is to your success, because you do want to run through the finish line to a successful new job, correct?

In a serious job search, you need to faithfully call at least four new contacts per day for three months.

If you do, the law of averages will work in your favor and you will most likely receive interviews and an acceptable offer. Now you know why names and their phone numbers are your most important commodities. Do the math. If you do not faithfully call those numbers of people, it will take you longer to find a job—unless you are very lucky.

During late winter 2017, I coached a talented System Administrator who had recently been laid off by his company. It took this Husband and Dad a few weeks to overcome his grief from losing his job far enough to begin calling and developing his network. Once he began contacting people, he shifted from zero calls to 6 to 7 calls per day. By the 60-day mark, he had 2 offers. He accepted the better offer and now loves his new job—and his new company loves his work!

Now it is time to clarify one small and very important piece of information. Note that I said call, not e-mail. Companies are doing much better protecting their networks from outside attacks and spam e-mails. Your contact may not receive your e-mail. On the other hand, they may see that you sent an e-mail but are so busy they didn't have time to respond immediately—and it was buried in their mass of email. I have been that person. Wasn't the road to hell paved with good intentions?

When you call your first contacts, tell them the reason for your call (networking) and ask if you can take a minute to tell them about your background. Now give them your "Here I Am!" speech. Then ask them whom they recommend that you talk with next. I guarantee that if you just ask them if they have an opening at their company, their kneejerk response 98 percent of the time will be

"No." Try to get at least four or five people's names and numbers from each person you call. These are your warm referrals. They may say they don't know anyone. Then ask, "Whom do you know at ABC company?" or, "Do you know anyone who lives in New England (or anywhere)?" Asking the latter question may help you get to a different part of the country without knowing anyone there yourself.

Remember six degrees of separation—by conducting six directed conversations, you may reach anyone in the United States.

What is a "warm referral?" When someone calls you, and says that a friend or business acquaintance gave them your name and number, you are more open to receiving the call, right? Not only that, you do not want to disappoint your friend, so you try to help that caller. That's why you seek warm referrals. A person you call out of the blue may not even take your call. If they do take your call, they may not be as likely to help you. (You still should make cold calls because they can lead to more warm referrals!)

Remember, in our current world, everyone is busy. They may want to chat with you but have now lost your contact information. Therefore if you have not received a reply from them, try to call prior to 8 AM, during lunch, or after 5 PM. You may just catch them at their desk. If not, don't leave a second message, simply try again another time.

Many times, someone I respected asked me to meet with a person who was out of work. I set aside some time and met with them. Why? I wanted to maintain the respect of my contact; and meet and exceed their expectations. Remember to give back when you have the opportunity.

When insurance companies hire young salespeople, they train them to call family and friends first. Why? Those typically are the least threatening calls. That's also why you should practice your new networking skills with friends and family. They will be happy to give you pointers, especially brothers and sisters...

All kidding aside, make your easy calls first and then work toward the more difficult cold calls. Most people will be willing to help you. Occasionally, someone may be having a bad day and act like a jerk. Understand that you may have been the 40th networking call they received that day, and they were nice to the first 38 people. If it makes you feel any better, hang up after saying good-bye, wait a couple of seconds, then pick up the phone and listen for the dial tone. If you hear the dial tone—and only if you hear the dial tone—you may say "Jerk!"

If you don't hear the dial tone, and still say "Jerk!", you may make my next book!

So, we have discussed many elements of networking but haven't discussed networking meetings. They are another way for you to meet people. As one of the organizers of the Park City Career Network, I can say we encouraged members to help each other. In many large cities and some smaller cities, there are groups helping people searching for their next positions. I have spoken to such groups around the country.

Many other organizations promote networking among the members. Your local Chamber of Commerce may offer "After Hours" meetings. Chamber members are generally given free admission and members of the community may join the "After Hours" for a small admission price. In my experience, these meetings have cliques and few people are really interested in true networking. But people are only as interested in you as you are in them. You have the time. Use it to meet new people. Imagine the little RecruiterGuy on your shoulder encouraging you to meet just one more person. He or she may be a person that you can help. Then they are more open to helping you.

Several years ago, I attended a conference. One of the presentations was by a noted author whose presentation was networking. During his presentation, he mentioned that when you are participating in networking meetings, totally focus on the person you're taking with. Obviously, if you are looking around the room while chatting with them, they know you really are not interested in their conversation.

After the presentation, I went up to thank him for his information. Ironically, as we were chatting, he was looking around the room. He personally lost a lot of credibility that day, but his point was spot on.

Treat people with respect. If you can make suggestions to help them, do so. If not, nicely excuse yourself and either leave or meet someone else. While "working a room," work very hard to maintain eye contact with the one person or group of people in your conversation. Do not look for your next conversation. Remember to pay attention. Sometimes a person will say something that triggers the right question from you and leads you somewhere totally unexpected—and worthwhile.

What else important could happen after you give your "Here I Am!" speech? They could ask you, "Are you interviewing with us?" Ahh, music to my ears! That's the response you may seek. If you are not interviewing with them, ask them who to contact within their firm or if they would be willing to introduce you. This is how you network your way into a job.

We've discussed some of the mechanics of networking. Now let's discuss the nature of networking and use some stories to illustrate it.

Networking can happen unexpectedly. It does not have to be scheduled, but you must be prepared to switch it on immediately. When you are out there meeting people, you could meet other new people.

In the 1980s when I was a contingent (fee-based) recruiter in Washington, D.C., one of my best clients was The Washington Post's IT group. In those days, The Washington Post had an excellent IT department, one of the best in the area. We had a great relationship. They knew that my referrals were right on target. One day I was downtown, not far from The Post building, meeting with another client. After the meeting, I stopped at a nearby restaurant for lunch. After I was seated, I began to let my mind and ears wander. Eventually, a conversation at the next table caught my attention. Obviously, the woman was an IT professional (in those days we called them data processing), and she was being interviewed by a recruiter. As their conversation proceeded, I decided that she would be a great fit for The Post. She had the perfect experience and attitude to succeed there. Since Katharine Graham was the publisher at The Post, there was no glass ceiling.

I decided that I was going to meet that candidate. Fortunately for me, my vigilance was rewarded. The other recruiter got up from the table, leaving her sitting there by herself.

Given the opportunity, I leaned over, apologized for listening in on her conversation, and asked if she would be interested in working for The Washington Post. She said, "Sure!" I asked her if she had an additional resume. She replied "No."

Then I asked her if she was available to interview the next morning at The Post. She replied that she was. I told her to fax her resume to me (no e-mail in those days) and to expect an interview at The Post at 9 the next morning. She agreed.

When she faxed her resume to me, I forwarded it to the manager at The Post. He called me back right away. I asked if the team was available to interview her the next morning. He said that he liked her background and would set everything up. When I called her back to set up the interview, I was so confident that she would receive an offer, I told her to expect an offer by 11 a.m. (Today, I may not be so over-confident!)

Employee 5.0

At 10:30 the next morning, the manager called me and was laughing. He said that he was going to extend her an offer. He had a problem—all three managers who interviewed her wanted her on their teams—and another manager was interviewing her right then. They were going to have to decide which team she would join.

The candidate called me about 11:15, right after leaving The Post. She was also laughing. She said her last interview was over at 10:50 a.m. The manager met with her and just before 11 a.m., he extended her an offer and she accepted. She asked how I knew. I replied that I knew my client that well.

A postscript to that story is that the other recruiter obviously found out that she accepted the job at The Post a couple of weeks later. He was very upset when she told him how we met, even wanted me to pay for lunch! He probably never left a candidate alone in a restaurant again after our incident. Neither did I!

Bottom line—prospects for networking surround you and you never know when one will strike up a conversation with you. Be prepared to accept that conversation.

As you develop your network, your conversations provide you with the opportunity to give your creative juices a shot! How? Listen very carefully to the other person after you ask them where you may be able to help them.

I always try to contribute ideas and suggestions when I have a conversation with anyone. It's good to ask, "Have you tried...?" Another good question is "What has been your biggest obstacle so far?"

As Employee 5.0, you need to become an expert networker. By that I mean, give and take!

Networking is perfect for you to grow professionally.

So far, we have not discussed the role of professional recruiters. You may expect a person who has been successful in that role since 1981 to trumpet the services of professional recruiting firms. Professional recruiters do play an important role in a job-search process; however, it is easier for a recruiter to earn a fee when a candidate is working than when he or she is out of work. Companies feel they can find people who are actively looking for jobs without paying a fee. Unfortunately, that professional's resume may be languishing in their Application Tracking System (ATS).

Therefore, it is best to develop a relationship with a professional recruiter while you are happily employed. Accept their calls warmly. If it seems they are calling too often, simply ask them to spread out the time between calls. Time is money to recruiters and they should accept your request gracefully. If they do find an interesting opportunity, feel free to explore it. If it is the right opportunity for you, you may find yourself in an exciting new position. This is the New World Order.

In my experience, many young professionals are reticent about receiving calls from professional recruiters. They are afraid someone will hear them talking with a recruiter. Understand that the executives in their company are having conversations with recruiters, some more actively than others. Recruiters contact executives both to recruit them for other executive positions that may interest them; and to provide candidates to your company.

Many times, I have developed professional relationships with candidates without being aware of any positions that would interest them at the time. I just wanted to get to know them, their interests, their skills, and personality. We would talk as they made impacts in their current position. We often discussed their excitement about something that went very well and the frustration when things weren't going well. Many times, a year or two passed before the perfect position became available. When I called them, we already had a relationship and the process proceeded smoothly to their next position. Rarely does this process happen quickly, but the example at The Post I told above demonstrates how unexpectedly and quickly it can happen.

Also understand a professional recruiter's responsibility is to the client. Clients pay recruiters to find the best possible match for them. Recruiters are not paid by the candidate. I wish I had a dollar for every time I've heard from a candidate that one recruiter or another "didn't do anything for me." Usually, I nicely say that it's not the recruiter's job to do something for them, but one will probably be happy to make some suggestions for their search.

It is important to notify everyone who helped you when you are successful finding your next job. Then ask them if there was any information that you may be able to give them because of your networking.

Some years ago in Cedar Rapids, Iowa, a young woman called me and asked if I could spend some time with her to discuss her job search. She had recently graduated from college and I had known her since her soccer playing days. I invited her to lunch at a restaurant where we could talk. We spent two hours discussing the job-search process and how to network her way to her first job. After lunch, she offered to pay for lunch. I told her that she could buy me a lunch after she started her first job.

After a few weeks, I received a call. She was excited to inform me that she had just accepted a job. She said, "Now I can buy you lunch!" A couple of weeks after her first check, we went to lunch. She was excited to tell me that my suggestions helped her. Why did her story make this book? She was one of the very few people who took my time and then got back to thank me for my time.

She has become a long-time friend and is successful in her career.

People in your network remember when you thank them—and when you don't. Think about the potential future impact.

Another potential source of networking is career fairs. I know some candidates refer to them as "cattle calls" and other not-so-nice names. But a career fair is a great place to meet people who work for companies that you may target, and to help you identify others that you did not know were in the area. I have spoken at more than 70 career fairs nationwide and worked a couple of hundred career fairs representing clients.

A skilled candidate may work a career fair as well as a teenager working Walt Disney World! Before the day of the career fair, look to see which employers plan to attend. Then go to their web site to check their open positions and any interesting press releases. They may not have open positions posted, but they may have announced an expansion—the job postings just haven't appeared yet. The fair organizers will usually post a map showing where the different companies will be located. Understand that they don't always show up where they are supposed to, but generally they will be where you expect.

On the day of the career fair, print 10 more resumes than you expect to need. Do not fold your resumes. Bring them in a portfolio where you can also take notes.

When you arrive at a career fair, they usually will ask you to register prior to entering. Sometimes they allow you to register electronically and use a memory stick to load your resume into their system. Many times, they forward all resumes to the companies that participate in the fair.

Now, I am going to give you the secret to working a career fair. It is one that every teenager knows when "working" an amusement park or a ski resort. People are wonderfully consistent. Typically, they stop at the first booth that interests them. They may even stand in a line there. Meanwhile, the people manning the booths in the back are lonely. Unless a company that interests you in front has no candidates, go directly to companies that interest you in the back of the hall. Depending on the size of the hall and the number of companies, you have about 10 minutes before other people join you. These 10 minutes can be very valuable because everyone is fresh. Later in the day, the recruiters who would rather be anywhere else may ignore you—pretty strange, huh? I've seen them pull up stakes a couple of hours early. Usually, that's when I meet the most interesting candidates because they were working earlier!

Would you like another secret? Introduce yourself to other job seekers. You may have run across something not interesting to you but interesting to them. Karma works! Somehow, you will benefit.

As you work a career fair, it is easy to tell which companies are experienced in dealing with candidates at one. It also gives you a sense for the company. For instance, prior to a career fair when I am representing my clients, I walk through the hall just prior to the opening of the doors. As Recruiter-Guy, I want to know who my true competition is for good candidates. Typically, they have arranged their booths to be welcoming to candidates. Other companies keep their tables between them and the candidates. That is commonly referred to as a barrier. Many times, how the booth is set also is a good indication of their culture. Are they open, or are they closed? Are they welcoming or not?

Generally, I try to attract one or more of my clients' managers to the fair to work with me. It is a great opportunity for them to see some of the quality of available candidates in the community and possibly even interview one or two of them. When a sharp candidate approaches, I invite them inside the booth, listen to their "Here I Am!" speech, look at their resume and then make a quick decision how to proceed. If they are a potential candidate for the manager who is with me, I excuse myself from the candidate for a minute to speak with the manager. The manager will look at the resume. If we agree to proceed, I suggest that the manager take the candidate to a nearby restaurant to interview. The manager is happy for an excuse to leave the booth, and the candidate is excited to have an interview so quickly. It's a win-win! More than one person has been hired that way.

Remember to pay attention as you work the career fair.

In 1996, I was working with a De La Rue subsidiary in Iowa. My tablecloth had De La Rue and the logo on both the front and on top of the table. I was in Des Moines, meeting candidates at the career fair that day. Toward the end of the day when things were slowing down and there were no candidates in front of me, a sharply dressed young man was walking past me. I stepped out and asked him what he was looking for. He said, "You probably don't have what I'm looking for." I asked again what he sought. He said, "Positions in Europe." I asked him why he was walking past a company named De La Rue. I forwarded his resume to corporate headquarters in the UK.

The primary tools of networking are your list, your "Here I Am!" speech and your perseverance. There is one more very important attribute that comes into play while networking: a positive mental attitude. People do what you expect them to do; therefore, if you expect them to blow you off, your self-fulfilling expectation will cause you to say something that causes them to blow you off. Always make calls with a smile on your face and the expectation of success. It will greatly improve your success rate.

Now you are moving forward on your search. You are beginning to gain some success and momentum! Can interviews be far behind? You have graduated from the early items of your checklist. They are now your responsibility.

Job Search PROCESS Checklist

Preparing for Your Interviews

- ✓ Review the examples of the situations that required your skills. After thinking about your examples over the last few days, are there better examples that you can use? As you are researching companies, new examples will continue to flow into your mind if you allow them. Again, the format is to discuss the situation and what you did as the result of the situation. Then discuss what happened as the result of your influence or direct action for each skill or attribute that demonstrates your skill. **People remember stories, not skill lists.** These stories are important to relate during your interviews.

- ✓ Develop a list of your positive, measurable impacts over the past 10 years, with focus on the last five years. List them from the most recent impacts backward. Remember the **4 W's**—What was the challenge? What was your response? What was the result? What did you learn?

- ✓ **If you still have old annual reviews, read them for impacts that you may have forgotten.** Both tasks prepare you for impressive interviewing!

- ✓ As you network, faithfully add new names to your spreadsheet and note how they may be related to other connections. Also ensure that you are only adding them once. More than one person may refer you to someone.

- ✓ You have developed your resume, "Here I Am!" speech and brand as a candidate.

- ✓ You have begun talking with people (networking). **Track your results. Remember, you are in a sales process. Working in a sales process, it is important to know your numbers.** While networking, it is important to track how many calls (phone and personal) you make per day. Then track the results of each call (Think baseball statistics—track measurable activity). To maintain a positive mental attitude, it is important to know your averages.

For instance, it is important to know that for every three calls you make, you have one conversation. For every five conversations, you get a personal meeting. For every three personal meetings, you set up an interview. For every two interviews, you receive an offer. That means 90 calls can yield an offer. If you make four calls per day, you can earn four offers over the course of 90 days.

This becomes your law of averages. Develop a spreadsheet to track:

- ✓ How many calls with no answers/left messages?

- ✓ How many conversations per day?

- ✓ How many names received in each conversation?

- ✓ How many phone conversations created a personal meeting

- ✓ How many of those meetings set up interviews?

- ✓ How many interviews resulted in offers?

- ✓ How many offers resulted before one was accepted?

Analyze your results. Does it feel that your networking should yield more interviews? If so, where do your metrics seem to be lower than you expect?

1. Is your "Here I Am!" speech passionate about your experience and accomplishments? Or are you simply reciting it? If so, create a script that you may read with excitement and enthusiasm!

2. Is your resume a sea of bullet points instead of your responsibilities in a paragraph and bullet points for accomplishments? As you develop your averages, you may adjust activity to speed up interviews or slow down interviews.

Determine where your numbers seem low. Then adjust. The tweaks may not need to be large changes. Possibly simply small tweaks. Many times during a job search, you will find the need to tweak approaches; and definitely, your resume to best fit the company's needs and culture.

Important—many candidates fall into the trap of shutting down their networking activities as soon as they begin an interviewing process. They are so certain that their networking efforts are done, they quit doing the things that made them successful. Understand that your first interviews may or may not result in offers. You may accept those offers, or you may turn them down for many reasons.

- ✓ **Redouble your networking efforts while participating in an interviewing process.** Success creates more confidence. Additional confidence creates better results.

- ✓ Remember your goal is to find positions that you love so much that you are excited to receive compensation for your impacts. You want days to fly by. You want to make positive, measurable impacts and have fun.

- ✓ Intense networking only ends after you start your next position. Then you continue to contribute to your networks but do so outside of Prime Time in consideration for your new employer/business.

- ✓ Begin a list of references. Decide which references are best to discuss which successful experiences.

Now that you know how, good luck networking!

Prior to discussing the interview process, let's address the importance of internships and co-op programs for college students in their search for their first professional job. All the work prior to this Step also applies to college students preparing to move into full time, professional positions.

This is one of those areas in the book where the experienced professionals may move directly to Step 10—"Impressive Interviewing."

I Am a Professional!

I GOT THIS!

STEP 9

Benefits of Internships and Co-Ops in Your Job Search

During the dot.com boom, a client was a very successful Silicon Valley technology firm. One of the founders, an alumnus of Rice University in Houston, Texas, often told me that college recruiting and internships gave his company "access to the brightest and the best minds while we can still afford them." We successfully recruited Rice University graduates for software engineering positions and undergraduates for internships at his firm. We also successfully recruited graduates and undergraduates from Brown University, UCLA, Purdue University, and the University of California—Berkeley. One of my responsibilities was to help the client develop its formal internship and co-op programs, and help the client develop a program to house those interns in the extremely expensive Silicon Valley real-estate market.

Today's college students are more astute than the students of the past—and luckier, too. In the past 30 years, internships have evolved into doing real work within the field the student has targeted. Previously, internships may have simply been a filing job in the right area. Because companies are leaner, and more filing is done electronically by individuals on the corporate network, companies want interns performing tasks that deliver measurable results. This provides students a wonderful opportunity to apply their knowledge in a work setting.

In the past, colleges and universities required the employer to take time weekly to report in depth on the intern's activities to call a job "an internship." That's fine if the supervisor has time; however, most supervisors are already working near their limits. This amount of reporting just discouraged the hiring of interns. Colleges and universities now have adjusted their reporting expectations to encourage the hiring of student interns. Now companies hire interns, teach them how to carry out their tasks and under supervision let them do their job. They expect results. At the end of the internship, there is typically an evaluation.

Students: Understand that you are being evaluated daily as you work.

You may not receive the feedback, but the team is constantly observing your work, work ethic and attitude to determine if you are a future fit. They want you to succeed, but if they perceive you as someone with a poor attitude, they will begin to cut their relationship time with you.

What is the value of a summer internship instead of a "summer job"? Sometimes a summer job can pay better than an internship; that is certainly attractive to a student paying his or her way through college. Generally, those summer positions are construction jobs, restaurant servers or manufacturing line positions.

A summer internship gives the student valuable training and insight into a field of interest.

Another important benefit is that you may decide that you really are not interested in that field or working at that company. It's better to change fields while in college than wait until you have graduated and are working; you may be able to change your course direction and degree to the new major.

I paid my way through Assumption College. Toward the end of my Junior year, I decided that my major in Psychology would not make me happy. On the other hand, I needed to complete my college education at the end of Senior year. Since my goal was to complete my education in 4 years, my first research was to determine which major's courses had almost enough credits to graduate. That major was English. Then, I determined that taking 2 English courses at The University of California, Santa Barbara, and a focus on English courses Senior year would suffice. By the way, since I lived in Maryland there was the hitchhiking adventure to get to summer class (but that is another book…). With some planning, you may be able to do the same.

This is a great time to practice as Employee 5.0—a person who has decided to take control of their career, not become dependent upon the largesse of the company to determine their growth and promotions. Generally, after the first 5 years, promotions and increased pay begin to slow as salary compression begins to grind progress to a halt. The 5.0 Employee knows the way to increase their salary is to be promoted internally—or to move to a position within a new company where they gain new skills.

The most important benefit of a successful internship is that you decide the field is for you. You demonstrated your abilities and work ethic to a company that is now interested in hiring you when you graduate. You may call this "Advanced Networking", or "Try before you buy."

What is the difference between an internship and a co-op? Generally, a co-op is a more formal program with a specific company. I usually see co-ops used more in the engineering or hard science areas. When you work in a co-op program, beginning in your junior year you will work a semester and attend class a semester. You will be paid for your work, but don't expect full-time compensation. The expectation is that the co-op will give you ever-increasing exposure and responsibilities. It will usually postpone your graduation into the following year. An internship generally occurs during summer breaks, but some are structured to continue as part-time positions or during semester breaks.

At the end of either program, you are either interested in the company and its work or you aren't. If you do a great job (depending on the economy), you will probably receive a job offer. As a candidate, this is the best offer to accept. You know your manager (typically). You know the company and the work. You enjoy working there.

One of my clients was an executive for a financial services company. He began interning at the company the summer of his sophomore year of college. He returned after his junior year and had another successful internship. During his senior year, he was offered a job there following graduation. He grew in the company for 25 years and was a vice president there when we last worked together.

It is not unusual for students to experience that same kind of success using the internship to find a job and later succeeding within the company. Many companies use their internship programs as a recruiting tool. It is a great way to "try out" students to determine if they are a match for the company in several ways:

- ✓ Proper skills or the ability to learn them quickly

- ✓ Proper cultural fit

- ✓ Ability to work as a team member

- ✓ Already have experience working with members of team and being accepted as a member of the team (very valuable!)

- ✓ Demonstrating the ability to make impacts given the proper corporate training

- ✓ "Selling" the student to work for the company by giving them challenging and fun assignments

A recent college graduate who has a successful internship at a company is more likely to be hired by that company than a student who is applying there without that experience. This method of recruiting is more valuable than the traditional sourcing and interviewing method.

The manager and company truly know the person they are hiring. Additionally, the candidate (student) also knows what to expect. It is a win-win.

Most colleges and universities have a career services or student professional development center on campus.

These professionals work very hard to attract well-known and locally attractive companies to recruit on campus. They work with interested students to prepare for their searches for internships and post-graduate jobs. Understand that while software or nursing or sales may be your field of interest, people who work in career services or professional development are passionate about your future success.

Speaking to you as a recruitment professional, I recommend that you heed their advice. Understandably, it is the nature of some students to discount the skills of the career-development professionals. You have been taught to question results and opinions as part of your college education.

There is also the adage about the prophet not receiving respect at home. It is not unusual for you to discount the abilities of people you see daily. Then listen to other people who are introduced to you as experts—and provide the same advice.

Remember that College Career Services Professionals have worked with hundreds or thousands of students and many companies in their years advising students on proper career searches. They have seen the mistakes students made that negatively affected their job searches. You haven't seen those mistakes, and may be about to make one. Take advantage of their knowledge and experience to accelerate your search.

Career Services Professionals usually begin to coach freshmen and try to reach them in the first semester of that year. Why so early? Generally, the most attractive internships become available in December and are offered in February. Those companies are trying to identify the "cream of the crop" early so they can lock them into an internship. Internships are more difficult to find between freshman and sophomore years, but persistent convincing freshmen can find them. After sophomore year, companies have more of your college experience to measure your ability to learn (grades) and will question you on your work experience; therefore, sophomores and juniors are more attractive as intern candidates.

Of course, you are now saying, "What work experience? How am I expected to get work experience if I need work experience to get it?" Good questions. Did you work in high school or part-time in college? It doesn't need to be in your field of interest. McDonald's, Wal-Mart, and Target are proud of the alumni who worked for them while in school. You made impressions on your manager. You know if they are good or bad impressions. Many high school students work very hard in their part-time positions. Others may not be as enthusiastic.

How does the Employee 5.0 model fit within internships? As Employee 5.0, you are the person who works to exceed expectations. Your goal is to make impacts for the companies where you work—doesn't matter if you are working at McDonald's and upselling at the counter (Do you want fries with that?) or if you are an intern in a large financial services company. This is where you develop and practice a strong work ethic. High school and college jobs are where people generally develop their work ethic—or not. Build your reputation as the "Go To Person" on a team.

If you worked hard, went above and beyond what was expected, and had great attendance, your chances of receiving a positive reference from your current manager goes way up.

Keep in mind that some managers are not allowed to provide references; or they may be angry that you are considering a move. However, most are more than willing to help you. If a manager congratulates you on an internship well done, feel free to ask them for a letter of recommendation where they may cite some of your impacts and work ethic.

When I was consulting on college recruiting with an avionics company, an engineering manager told me, "I will hire a college graduate with a 3.4 GPA who had an appropriate internship before I hire a grad with a 4.0 GPA. Why? If you are only studying, you are expected to earn a 4.0 GPA. I like graduates who work during college because they learn how to perform in the work environment." I cannot improve on that statement.

Now you know "why" to work summer internships while in college. Let's discuss how to find and be hired for an internship.

Obviously, your career services or professional development office is the place to start.

Develop a relationship with the professionals in that office early in your college career. Work with them so they know what kinds of internships or co-ops are particularly interesting to you. It would be wise to volunteer in that office during its peak times. They can teach you more about the job search process, and you never know who you will meet when you are volunteering.

Remember, companies are trying to develop stronger relationships with schools where they had previous success. A representative of the company may be there when you are in the office. You want the career services staff to recommend you when a company calls and asks for recommendations.

Listen to the career-services professionals' advice on companies where you should apply for an internship.

- ✓ Ask them who has hired interns from your college/university program in the past.

- ✓ What kind of experience did those interns have?

- ✓ Research to determine companies where you would like to intern.

- ✓ Ask career services if any of your school's alumni either work at or sponsor internships at those companies.

- ✓ Do your parents work in companies that have appropriate internships? Do they know the hiring manager? Can you apply there?

- ✓ Find out where recent grads from your program are working and contact them. They often keep their college e-mail addresses for some time after they graduate.

- ✓ Establish a professional profile on LinkedIn and search for other alumni at companies that interest you.

- ✓ Ask career services if there are older grads from your program who are executives at an appropriate company. They may be willing to create an internship for the right person.

- ✓ As you are working this list of suggestions, begin a list of names of people you will network with outside of your college/university.

- ✓ Whose parents do you know? Can they help you find an internship in your field?

- ✓ If you are active in your religion, go to your religious leader and ask who they know who may be willing to help you find an internship.

If you hit dead ends with these solutions, return to **STEP 8: "Effective Networking to Your Next Position!"** and follow those steps. Persistent students prepare and are determined to succeed.

A couple of years ago, I met an industrious college junior at Assumption College in Worcester, MA, who was very interested in an internship with a well-known New England financial services company. He kept getting noncommittal comments when he asked for his internship status. Finally, one Friday morning he went to their offices in a nearby city. He told security that he was a student who wanted to interview for a summer intern program. As his luck would have it, another student who was offered an internship had just called to decline. This junior was interviewed and received an offer for his internship that day. Timing is everything! And so is polite persistence!

During this process, pretend that you are a consultant offering your services to a firm for the summer. Use all your different talents to land an interview for your internship. Be creative. Talk with as many people you can.

If you find an internship that does not interest you, either let your career-services office know or go directly to another student you know that may be qualified and interested. Remember, networking is all about helping others in your network.

Now let's discuss your communications skills briefly. I know many college students are trying to replace human contact with texting contact. It can be a timesaver. I am also intimately aware of mobile recruiting applications from the corporate side.

Here is the danger of trying to communicate solely by e-mail and text: neither enables you to efficiently describe the tone of your message. Smiley faces don't cut it in a professional world.

The recruiting/interviewing process is a sales process. The candidates who understand this concept are the ones who are most successful growing their careers. **The sales process is a relationship building process.** Remember that the hiring process tends to be a cross-generational environment where people of all ages are involved.

The nature of seasoned executives tends to dictate older management. Obviously, there are highly successful young managers—and those managers tend to remain successful throughout their careers.

Bill Gates is a wonderful example of a person who was successful at a younger age. Eventually, those successful young managers become successful older managers, and you need to be able to communicate with them at their level to be successful with them either as an employee or as a vendor supplying them.

Therefore, take the time to communicate with the managers and human resources professionals directly. If you don't, you run the risk of being eliminated by your competition. Also, no job is truly yours until the day you start. So, you need to communicate all the way through the process until your start date. Offers may be rescinded. Do not assume that a hiring manager will accept text messages as a replacement for conversations.

Many times, I have observed candidates when I thought one or another was best for the position, and then watched that person lose out when someone else was introduced at the last minute.

Enjoy your internships/co-ops! This is a great way to continue to learn the new workplace and apply the new concepts that you have been taught. Also remember, corporate e-mail systems are not to be used for distributing jokes or pictures. Because they are the property of the company, network administrators may read your e-mail to ensure it is business related. **If these lines saved you from embarrassment or firing, then this book is worth it.**

**Job-Search PROCESS Checklist—
Internships/Co-ops**

- ✓ Meet with your career services/professional development services professionals as soon during freshman year as is possible to discuss your current career aspirations.

- ✓ Work with them to develop a plan to work while in college to develop internships or co-op programs.

- ✓ Especially during freshman year, offer to volunteer for career services events—for instance, career fairs. You never know who you may meet that may lead to an internship. You are beginning to build your reputation as a hard worker.

- ✓ Attend the career services meet-and-greet events. Put yourself in position to be successful.

- ✓ The best way to find an internship (and later a job) is to network your way to one.

- ✓ Remember to communicate "the old-fashioned way" with older managers. While it is part of your normal communication skills, not everyone is familiar with or interested in texting. You may be able to "teach" them its advantages, but only after you develop a working relationship with them.

- ✓ When you interview with managers and human resources, ask for their business cards.

- ✓ Remember to follow up internship interviews with handwritten thank you notes. Your competition rarely writes thank you notes for interviews. It is a successful best practice for the rest of your career.

- ✓ Once in your internship, apply yourself enthusiastically and learn everything you can.

- ✓ Remember to develop the habits of Employee 5.0—take charge of your career. Accept other experienced people's advice and assistance—But—do not depend on them.

Good luck! Enjoy this new experience that will prepare you for your career.

Now let's learn how to be an impressive interviewee!

I Am A Professional!

I GOT THIS!

Make this your mantra going forward!

Now let's discuss Step 10: Impressive Interviewing

STEP 10

Impressive Interviewing

You have now had the opportunity to decide what position you want to target. You have set a goal that stated the job and when you will be want to start working. You have developed your resume so it can be tailored for each position that you are targeting. You have networked and spent a little Non-Prime Time responding to Internet postings (no more than 10 percent of your search time), and now you have an interview scheduled!

At the time that the interview is scheduled, ask if the company can send you the application. It is far better to complete the application when you have the information handy—and you are not under the stress of the interview. Tell the truth on your application and in your interview. (Remember the stories in Step 3.)

I coach my clients (companies) that recruiting is sales. We have discussed that the job search is sales! Remember the spreadsheet comparison in Step 2? It is important that you understand this concept while searching for a job. What are you selling? You are selling your skills and abilities! If you haven't developed any skills over the years, why would someone want to hire you?

You have worked hard to get to this point. For me, interviewing is fun. I look at it as another networking opportunity where I may be able to help a manager or company benefit from knowing me. **I define an interview as a conversation with a purpose—and both sides have the purpose of deciding if this relationship is best for them.**

This is a good time to warn you about a typical candidate behavior.

When a candidate schedules an interview, they often stop networking. Never stop networking!

This position may not be the right one. You do not want to have to restart your networking process and lose the momentum you've developed. So, set time aside every day to continue your networking efforts. In sales, action begets action; therefore, you may find more opportunities while exploring the first one. Wouldn't it be nice to have several offers to choose from? Timing doesn't always work perfectly, but sometimes it comes close. Remember, you are looking for the job that is so enjoyable that you can't believe they are also paying you!

It is the summer of 2017. One of the executives that I coached was laid off and was looking seriously for his next opportunity to make impacts. Up until early July, he had several solid interviews without an offer. Then he had back to back interviews with CEO's in different parts of the country. Both were very interested in his background. One company was headquartered in the Midwest and the position was in Arizona. The second company was in the Southeast. The second company brought him and his wife to interview. The executives and wives took them to dinner after they arrived. The wives spent time with his wife while he interviewed—nicely done!

The first company made him an offer first— on Thursday with the stipulation that he accept or decline by Noon Central time on Monday. Oh, they did not send him to the plant where he would move nor did they tell him what the relocation package would look like—just "to be determined". The second company informed him that they would extend him an offer on Tuesday. As you can see, it was close—but the timing was a little off. The executive called me on Sunday evening, asking for guidance. We discussed both companies and how both treated him. Up until the first company required him to decide by Noon Monday, both treated him very well. I reminded him that he did not have all the information he needed to make a go—no go decision by Monday. My recommendation was to request a trip to the plant in Arizona to meet the staff who would report to him; and request the relocation benefits. I also coached him that the company was "recruiting" him now. This should be when they show their best side. If they decided to be offended when he made these reasonable requests, imagine how they will treat him once he is employed. He followed my suggestion.

Fortunately, the first company showed its true face; and rescinded his offer. On Tuesday, the second company called him and told him how excited they were to extend him an offer. They forwarded the offer letter prior to the conversation so he would have time to digest the offer and develop any questions. When they spoke, he asked if they could increase his relocation package to reflect the cross-country move. They analyzed his request and approved it.

This was the tale of two companies. He has already started and loves his new position! This is what I wish for you!

RecruiterGuy.com Series

I have an important little secret for you.

As the result of working with several thousand managers since 1981, I can tell you that every single manager has one common feeling regarding interviewing, and it does not matter how skilled they are as an interviewer.

Every single manager is rooting for you to succeed during your interview.

Outside of recruiting teams, most managers dislike the recruiting and interviewing process. They want to spend their time managing their team and making impacts in their fields, not going through dozens of resumes and interviewing strangers. Once they have chosen a slate of candidates to interview, they hope at least one qualifies to work with them. You can understand why they do not want to begin the process again.

Some managers look at this process as an opportunity to improve their team. Those are the great managers who really know how to grow a high-performance team. Their interviews will be strenuous as they try to determine if you have the right skills and attitude.

Therefore, once you have been invited to interview, the odds slightly raise in your favor that you'll get a job there.

Now, it is up to you to earn the respect of the manager and/or management team. You earn this respect through preparation for the interview. If you try to skate through an interview, you may just continue skating out the door because you will lose the respect of the manager.

In Step 1, I suggested that you develop a skills inventory (those skills that you do well). Prior to an interview, take time to look at the inventory. For every skill with an asterisk, develop a succinct story that relates a time when you successfully used that skill and how it may apply to this position and company. Because you spent time researching the company, you have some knowledge of how these skills may be used to make impacts at this new company. Jot a few words down that will help you recall that example. Remember that often managers are taught to ask, "What is your greatest skill/talent?" This list helps you to prepare for those questions.

Why relate a story to demonstrate the skill? There are two major reasons: The first reason is that hiring managers look for proof that you have a skill. Simply responding that you have a skill is not an effective interviewing technique. Generally, that response will cause the interviewer to feel that you are trying to avoid the question.

The second reason is that **people remember stories**. This is important.

When I was on a recruiting contract with a major telecommunications firm, the managers were interviewing six candidates per day. Many times, they later referred to a candidate by "He/she was the candidate that told the story about..." Soon, another manager who interviewed candidates that day would chime in, "That's Sylvester!" And everyone agreed. Then one would ask to extend Sylvester an offer.

Research the company as you would if you were going to sell to it. What does its online marketing look like? What do its press releases say? If it is a public company, look at its financials. Print a copy of its job description or cut and paste it to your electronic pad. It is important to be an educated candidate. This research helps you develop better questions to ask the hiring manager. For instance, "On your web site, I saw that your company is... How is that going to impact your group?" "Is this job description an accurate representation of the job responsibilities?" "What are the three month, six month, nine month and twelve month goals for the position?"

You can learn much about a company before you interview—knowledge is power.

If you know someone who works there, give them a call to ask if they know anything about the position or what demonstrated skills the manager seeks.

In 1985, a bright, young applications programmer contacted me. He was interested in learning to be a systems programmer (working the bits and bytes of the operating system). Generally, that was a very tough transition. At the same time, I was talking with a Systems Programming Manager at Chessie (CSX Technology) in Baltimore. He was looking for a junior systems programmer. I suggested that he interview this person. He agreed to interview Doug the next week.

I set up the interview. During our conversation, I mentioned that Doug should go to the library over the weekend and research the Chessie Railroad and CSX Technologies. He did. The next week I received a call from the hiring manager. He laughed, and said, "He knew more about my company than I knew. If he can research like that for systems programming, he will be a great systems programmer!" Doug accepted his offer.

Knowledge is power!

You may decide during your pre-interview research that you do not want to interview with the company. If that is the case, it is best to make that decision earlier rather than later—and call them to let them know. It's OK. No point to waste people's time. If you decide to make that call, thank them for their time and tell them that you are looking for a position or industry that matches your goals more closely.

This does bring up a point. If you agree to interview, you have made a commitment to that manager, his or her team and anyone else involved. They have set time aside in their schedules to give you their total focus.

If you decide not to interview with a company for any reason, call and let them know. If you simply don't show, you burn more bridges than you can imagine.

I introduced a candidate to one of my clients. He was going to interview with the CEO. On the morning of his interview, he did not show. He did not call them, nor did he call me. You can imagine my feelings when the CEO called to let me know the candidate didn't show! When I finally reached him, he said that he heard the CEO was a nasty person and he "decided not to interview." I asked why he did not call me nor the client. He said that he "didn't feel like it." What bridges do you suppose he burned that day? Obviously, the CEO and any members of the management team who were going to interview him.

About 10 years later, this same candidate approached me to be introduced to my new "sexier" client. After asking him about his experience since I knew him before, I determined that he had not changed nor was his experience directly applicable. Therefore, I did not introduce him to my client. He complained directly to my client that I did not introduce him. When the vice president asked me why I chose not to introduce him, I told her the whole story. She was happy that I did not waste her time with this candidate. Now he had lost credibility with another leader in another company. This was in 2010.

Believe it or not, this person approached me yet another time in 2014 to introduce him to another client. Will. Not. Happen. Ever.

It is important to respect people's time whether you respect them or not.

Interview processes differ with each company. When someone calls out of the blue to phone interview you, ask them if you can set up a time for the conversation, even later that day. It will give you time to compose and prepare yourself mentally for the conversation. They understand that you may have something already going on when they call. They may call just to set up a phone screen where they are trying to determine whether you meet the minimum requirements. My phone screens tend to be more detailed because I want to be able to advise the manager who I feel are the strongest candidates—and why.

When I am working with employers, particularly if they have many resumes, I suggest that we develop a phone screen to determine who goes to the next level. While you may not interview with the manager in this phone screen, you need to take it seriously. The person conducting this screen, usually a corporate recruiter, is your current gatekeeper—and may be your best advocate. Treat them with respect. The questions they ask can help you get a better sense for the position and the direction of the company. Remember, it is important for you to be an active listener.

Did you realize that when you are paying attention, your brain is actually working harder?

Ask this person about the job description and the accountabilities of the position. Toward the end of the phone screen, ask how you can expect the process to move forward.

Now it is the day of the onsite interview. How do you prepare? Go through all your notes and the job description. Review the company's press releases to see if there is any late-breaking news that is valuable to you. You may want to add or change one of your short stories.

If you smoke, don't. Nonsmokers can smell smoke on your breath and your clothes. Don't kid yourself. I can smell smoke on clothing, even if you weren't the one smoking. Today, smoking can cost you a job offer. Like it or not, insurance research demonstrates that smokers are sick more often than non-smokers. Companies can select the candidates who are the best "fit" for their business. You make your own decisions.

If the job is an office or sales job, wear professional clothing: suit, tie, polished shoes. Women should wear conservative jewelry (no dangling earrings) and conservative cosmetics, if you decide to wear either. Beyond earrings, it is best not to show body piercings or tattoos in a professional office for your interview.

You have heard this before—**you have one opportunity to make a good first impression.**

It is natural for people to look at your clothing and accessories" and make judgments regarding your "fit" in an organization. I've heard candidates say, "If they don't like my beard/long hair/tattoos/piercings, that's tough. That's who I am." I accept that line of thinking. Just don't complain if the company feels another person is a better fit for your otherwise perfect job. Remember, the manager also has a right to determine if someone is a fit for their team.

One of my consumer product group clients hired a human-resource generalist. Their corporate culture shuns body piercings and tattoos. They inform candidates during the interviewing process that they are not acceptable. The candidate interviewed without a tongue stud; however, on her first day on the job, she was sporting a tongue stud. The vice president of human resources requested that she remove it. The new employee, who was on a customary 90-day probation, refused to remove it. That was also her last day.

A great book, if you have questions about dressing for an interview, is John T. Molloy's *New Dress for Success*. He researched professional dressing and how people reacted to different styles. I have recommended his books to candidates for more than 25 years because they are based on research and fact.

If it is an outside job—construction, for example—wear appropriate, clean business casual clothing to your interview. If the job is one that is with a company that values outdoor experience, wear appropriate clothing for the position.

I worked a career fair once where a candidate told his friends that he was so good, and companies were so desperate for candidates, he could even get a job offer if he walked around with a clown costume on. What an arrogant schmuck! He even dropped off his resume with companies. No offers for him then—nor probably later. His arrogance really stood out. By the way, the companies who received his resume shared his name with other companies.

Dress is important.

Beware of the food that you eat a couple of hours before your interview. Some food can make you gassy. (Or smelly!)

Once when we were interviewing IT professionals, the IT manager came to my office when her interview with a candidate was over. The manager said, "Don't ever put someone like that in front of me again!" I was startled. The candidate worked for a competitor and on the same types of systems. At that point, we did not know he was failing the technical test. I asked the manager what was wrong with the candidate. It seemed that shortly after he sat down, the poor guy began having gas problems. The manager had to open her windows when he left. Lesson learned.

If you will be even two minutes late, call ahead and tell your connection (HR or the hiring manager). They understand construction, accidents, flat tires, etc. Where did that courtesy go? Everyone has a cell phone now! (Speaking of cell phones, turn it off before you enter the building.) Respect other people and they will respect you.

When you walk into the office for your interview, treat everyone with respect.

Period. I generally ask everyone to tell me if the candidate was disrespectful. This is when you should be on your best behavior. Respect the receptionist and act professionally through your interviews. I have had candidates occasionally who felt they were too important to listen to requests the receptionist made. Those actions rarely go unnoticed; the receptionist will let people in the company know.

Occasionally, you will interview with a company that prefers candidates to complete and sign the application in their office. There have been times when a candidate refused to complete the application when the receptionist presented it. I'm really not sure what one expects to gain from that refusal. It sure isn't going to be a ringing endorsement. Prior to interviewing him, the HR manager "allowed" him to complete the application at her desk as she waited and worked on e-mail. That experience was probably a little uncomfortable... I don't believe he received an offer.

No matter your feelings about a company's recruitment processes, you can't do anything about them until you develop credibility inside the company. It is best to follow their processes no matter how backward—or elect to end the process. You do have choices.

Before we go into personal interviews, let's briefly discuss the different formats.

Most candidates are aware of the interview where you sit across the desk from the person interviewing you. It's strictly a "normal" one-on-one interview. The interviewer leads the interview and the candidate follows.

Another potential format is one candidate with a panel of interviewers. This is more stressful for candidates because you may have two or more people asking questions at the same time. How do you handle that format? Apologize to the second manager and focus on responding to one person and one question at a time. Once you respond to the first manager's question, turn to the second manager and ask them to please repeat their question. You want to give that question your total focus.

Another potential format is the competitive interview where you have multiple candidates facing multiple interviewers, generally one of whom is a psychologist. (While I have never participated in this format, I did suggest it once because I had a bad feeling regarding one of the potential candidates. His ALL CAPS EMAIL RESPONSE disqualified him; and we didn't have to spend the time interviewing him.) The competitive interview attempts to measure both your ability to handle a stressful meeting and at the same time work to create consensus with your responses. Executives look to see if you acknowledge other participants' best responses. They also are trying to get a sense for how you fit into the executive team. It is expensive and time consuming. Some CEOs swear by this format of interview to see how interviewing executives handle the stress of it and determine who is best for their team.

The interview process is where executive candidates may find a slightly different path to follow. Many companies conduct an in-depth vetting process that includes meeting with a psychologist, credit checks, higher level background investigation, and multiple interviews. Generally, the interviews are spread over several weeks while weeding out weaker candidates. Many times, a presentation to Executive Staff is required.

For the purpose of keeping things simple, let's focus on the more common one-on-one interview, possibly with several managers scheduled to meet with you. While you are in the lobby, check your cell phone one more time to ensure it is off.

There are different methods to interview candidates within different formats. To prepare you for these interviewing techniques, let's explore the different types of methods that you may experience. The 8 different methods are:

1. Behavioral Interviewing
2. One step questions
3. Two step questions
4. Silence
5. What is the same/What is different
6. Example

7   Echo

8   Yes/No

> ✓ Much has been written about **Behavioral Interviewing**. Some companies attempt to design the entire interview as a behavioral interview. People are wonderfully predictive. When backed into a corner, we attempt to solve a problem in the same manner where we found success in the past. The interviewer anticipates challenges the new employee will face in this position and structures a question that can give insight about how the candidate will handle it.
>
> For instance, let's assume that this is a call-center manager position with angry clients who escalate after getting unsatisfactory answers (for them). Here's a potential line of behavioral questions for a professional with call-center experience: "When you were a manager at XYZ Services Co., how did you handle angry clients who wanted to escalate a problem up the chain of responsibility? Can you give me a couple of examples when you were able to satisfy

the client?" After you respond they may ask, "Obviously, it is difficult to satisfy everyone. Please give me an example of a situation when you couldn't satisfy the client. Describe the situation, the actions that you took and the results. What did you learn from that situation?" You can tell that they are trying to determine how you will respond to those clients once you start working there. More importantly, they demonstrated the best way to create a story.

A follow-up question is generally the most effective way to probe a candidate's response to a behavioral question. There are several methods to probe the response. One way is to compliment them. "Congratulations on handling that very difficult situation! What experience from your past did you draw from to decide to take that path?"

Occasionally, it is good for the manager to change the line of questioning by asking a probing type of question where the interviewer is looking for a what, when, where or who response. **This is the one step question.** For instance, "Where were you working when you were trained to handle conflict?"

✓ It is best if the manager pays attention to your response to any question. **Asking a follow-up question (making this a two step question)** to your response of the probing question can provide more information that leads to understanding your motivations. An example follow-up question could be, "If you were receiving such valuable training at that company, why did you choose to leave?" Or they are looking for more information. They may want to see how much information you have absorbed in your research and interview, so they ask, "What positive, measurable impacts do you feel you could make in this position?"

✓ **One of my favorite techniques to use with sales professionals is to be silent** after they respond to a behavioral question, then nod my head or move my hand as if to say, "Please continue…" Then I see how much more information they will give me.

On several occasions, the sales candidate continued to talk for 20 minutes without asking me for a clarification. One candidate reached the 20-minute point and stopped dead in his tracks. He looked at me and said, "I just blew this interview, didn't I?" When you find yourself in this situation, simply ask the interviewer what additional information they are looking for, so your response may be focused to their need for information. An interview is not the time to enter the confessional, especially unknowingly.

✓ **When a manager wants to understand more about specific positions or situations that you have worked, they may ask you to compare one position or project to another.** "You said that the sale to XYZ Company was one of the most complicated sales you have closed. How did that compare to the one with ABC Company? How were they different? What did you learn from each sale?"

✓ **There are times that the interviewer may repeat some of the words from**

your answer to elicit a response. Your response to why you left a position could be, "I just didn't feel that my professional impacts were appreciated." The interviewer may respond, "Professional impacts?" They are giving you an opportunity to talk about your impacts; and at the same time are developing a better understanding of your motivations. A professional in this situation takes advantage by telling a story that discusses the **4 W's**—What was the challenge? What was your response? What was the result? What did you learn? It is good to create some stories where the outcome was not as expected. Then discuss what you learned and how you changed. **Important, humans remember stories far better than statistics.** Take advantage!

- ✓ I train hiring managers to ask open-ended questions. **Sometimes a yes or no response is fine.** Have you been convicted of a felony? Do you have a DUI on your driving record?

- ✓ When your resume contains broad statements regarding skills, you should expect a hiring manager to ask for examples to prove that you have those skills. Remember when you were building stories to demonstrate those skills in our first steps? Now you apply that lesson and give the best example from your repertoire of responses that suits their needs. For instance, perhaps in your resume you mentioned you had "excellent management skills." What does that mean? In comparison to whom or to what? Tell your story that discusses the success of the people you have managed.

It is important to be able to discuss your identified strengths and tell stories that demonstrate success with those skills. Try to pick skills that would make positive impacts in that position. **When you talk about your successes, you get excited and your face lights up!** If asked, it is also important to discuss areas that you need to improve and what you are doing to improve those skills. For instance, you may be terrified of speaking to a group. You have identified that as an area for improvement, so you join a local Toastmasters group to practice and improve the skill. Managers appreciate the fact you know where you need improvement and have taken the initiative to improve.

One client asked me to train a talented new human-resource representative how to interview. We chose an executive administrative assistant position that reported to a tough sales vice president. The rep combed through the resumes we sourced and picked the three she thought were best. When I looked at the stack, I concurred. She set up the appointments for the three candidates.

When each of them arrived, she introduced me to them. I mentioned that I was coaching the rep to improve her interviewing skills. I was going to sit on the other side of the conference room table from them. If we went through the entire interview without me asking a question, that was great. If I did ask a question, it was because I needed additional clarification.

The first two candidates and the rep did just fine. I did not feel the need to speak up. The third candidate was doing well until she was asked what her weakness was. The candidate said, "My weakness is that I like people too much." Well, that was the first time that I ever heard that as a weakness, so she received my full attention. She then went on to make her weakness a strength.

The rep was going to let her move forward. I decided to probe a little deeper. I excused myself and said, "Well, we were looking more for a skill you needed to improve. What you did was turn your weakness into a strength. I recognize that approach in interview coaching. Can you tell me what area you need to improve?" She responded that, "Another weakness is that I…" and proceeded to turn it into a strength. I replied that I understood how she was taking some attribute, discussing it as a weakness and then demonstrating positive results from that action or attribute.

Trying one more time, I asked, "This is an important support position to a vice president of sales. Are there any software classes where you would like to improve skills or any other area we could help you improve your skills?" Her response? "I am NOT a weak person!" She was right! However, she did not listen, either. I apologized profusely and turned the conversation back over to the rep. The rep recognized that the interview was essentially over at that point since we found her fatal flaw.

Remember that people remember stories. When you stop reading this book, will you remember all the principles that we discussed? Probably not. Will you remember the stories? The ones that resonated with you will probably remain in your memory for a while; therefore, prepare to tell the stories that best represent your skills and abilities to get the job done.

Take the time to practice answering these different types of questions. (There are sample questions in Appendix B on Page 323.) Have someone ask you different questions from all of the different interviewing techniques. Just as a shortstop in baseball practices fielding each type of grounder, line drive and pop-up time and again so they are confident in a game, practice interviewing so you can recognize what the interviewer is looking for in your response. A key way to build a relationship with a hiring manager and team is to demonstrate confidence during your interview.

Here comes your first interviewer. Approach with confidence, appropriate eye contact and a friendly smile. Give them a firm handshake—don't break their fingers, just firm. Never give anyone a wet fish handshake! Yuck! It just says so many bad things about you—lack of confidence is among them. It used to surprise me when a woman gave me a firm handshake. Now women seem to be taught the importance of a firm handshake and do so more consistently than some men.

Appropriate eye contact means to look directly at the interviewer, but this is not a staring contest. A nice friendly smile is appropriate. It is fine to accept an offer of water. Water is nice because it can help settle your throat should it tighten. Remember that coffee may leave your mouth dry and with that nasty used coffee smell. I know. I drink coffee.

When you go into the office or conference room, wait until your interviewer indicates where you should take a seat before sitting. *Once I had a manager candidate that I was interviewing go behind the desk when we entered the office. I smiled and said, "I can see what side of the desk you are used to sitting." He laughed and said, "Oops!" He was fine. I let him remain in that seat for our interview. We offered the job and he accepted.* Generally, it is better that the interviewer gestures toward the appropriate seat.

When you have a cup or container of water, ask for a coaster before placing it on a desk. It's not good form to stain a nice desk, but you would be remembered…

In preparation for your interviews, visualize the potential structure of your interview. There generally is a warm-up period. It is followed by the meat of the interview, and then the point where the manager has decided; and asks if you have any further questions. Professionals pay attention during interviews, and sense when you are moving into the different phases. Many times, you may know if the manager is definitely interested in you. The manager may just tell you so and ask when you can start. They may be subtle, but still let you know there is interest in your candidacy.

When I present "The Secrets of a Successful Job Search," I tell the audience that a good interview is like a racquetball game. Prior to playing a racquetball game, you have a short warm-up session. It gives an experienced player an opportunity to test the opposing player. Just as in the racquetball warm-up, the first questions in the interview are very easy—"Tell me a little about your experience." Generally, the interviewer asks this question while they are reading your resume (sometimes for the first time). This is an appropriate time to use your "Here I Am!" speech. Then they may ask a little about your most-recent job. Now that you are warmed up, a skillful interviewer will begin the behavioral questions mixed in with the specific skill questions.

One or more of the questions may be directed toward your relationship with your previous managers. If you are so inclined, this would be a great opportunity to absolutely slam them. Don't do it! Just be happy to characterize your relationship as "professional." If you say negative things about a previous manager, what happens?

The hiring manager wonders if the problem was the manager or you? Then they wonder what you will say about them in a couple of years; this is not the path you want them on. Don't lie and say you had a wonderful relationship if it wasn't.

Remember, the previous manager may be called as a reference. When the previous manager asks the hiring manager how you characterized the relationship and the reply is "professional," they will probably return the favor.

Remember to ask good, informed questions based on your notes and based on what the manager has told you.

I once worked with a senior manager who laid out a situation in her interview. If the candidate did not ask a specific question, she would not extend an offer to them. You need to be an active listener. (She never shared the specific question with me.) If you can focus on the hiring manager and their questions, it is a good idea to jot down some notes. These may help you develop questions. Remember, if you do not understand how an organization is set up or why a company has a specific process or why something that you heard sounded wrong, ask the interviewers a question to clarify your thinking. That is more than okay; it is expected.

Part of your job during the interview is to attempt to build a professional relationship with the people who conduct the interview. Remember, if someone is interviewing you, they generally have input on whether you will be hired. Most hiring managers want to feel that you will jump into their canoe and paddle upstream with them. You build that relationship through active listening and asking good questions—and through the stories you relate that demonstrate you have done this in the past.

Look at pictures and certificates or degrees on their office wall. Imagine your good fortune if you happen to note they graduated from the same college as you. This gives you an immediate relationship with them. Paying attention to your surroundings may give you clues about the company culture and the people working in that culture. It was not that long ago when there were photos of beautiful women (not family members) in guy's cubes—and it was fine—and probably was a big warning sign for women candidates. *When I visit a new potential client, I take mental snap shots. Are employees surfing the Net or playing games online during work? Are they smiling as I walk through the offices? Is there music playing? Could I live with it as I work? Are employees meeting in nooks around the office to discuss business? Are they in more formal Conference Rooms? What are the expressions of the employees in the meeting? Bored or Engaged?* Understanding the corporate culture is an important element in your determination of a potential fit for you.

During the interview, it is a good idea to take notes. Focus on the challenges and where you may be able to make impacts. It is good to discuss an area where it is critical for you to make an impact. Once you feel the manager is comfortable that you will make that impact, ask him or her if he or she agrees you will be able to make progress there. This reinforces in their minds that they have found someone who can help solve problems. Isn't that what people are paid for—solving problems? If he agrees, then write it down. If not, you now know that you must overcome that objection before you receive an offer. Ask if you can return to that question or situation and discuss it further. At this point you are consulting with him. Ask for more information and then use an experience from your past that demonstrates you can make that impact or know how to solve the problem.

Your posture during an interview is very important.

If you lean back in your chair, it appears you lack interest in the conversation. Sit toward the edge of your chair and sit straight up.

When you make a point, lean forward to demonstrate the importance of that point.

This action also demonstrates your confidence in making the point. This confidence, shown by a professional, gives you the edge over someone who is not confident. Over the years, many candidates have lost opportunities because managers felt they were either lazy or not interested. Their posture gave the bad impression.

I've alluded to you asking the hiring manager what the three month, six month, nine month, and twelve month goals were for the position. Again, you want this information because:

1. The skills necessary to be successful in that position in the first year become crystal clear.

2. The title of the position and the job description do not give you the level of information you need to decide if the position truly interests you.

3. The goals give you and the manager an opportunity during the interview to discuss the challenges they expect you to overcome. They also give you the opportunity to demonstrate you can perform the job successfully. If you feel the manager has questions regarding your ability to do this job, and you feel one of your references can answer those questions for both of you, feel free at this point to offer their name and

phone number to discuss your experience at a previous company. Let your reference know to expect the call and why someone is calling.

4 During your meetings after you are hired, you may use these goals to discuss progress and challenges and to ask for advice. At your annual review, there should be no surprises for either of you.

Once I was doing some career counseling with a CFO. As we were discussing the interview and salary-negotiating process, I suggested that he mention that until he knew what the accountabilities were for the CFO position, he could not put a value on the position. He replied that if he interviewed a CFO and the CFO candidate didn't know what the accountabilities were for that position, he would show him the door. My reply? "So, what you are saying is the responsibilities for the CFO position for General Electric are the exact same as the CFO position at a telecom startup—and both positions have the exact same accountabilities as those in a financially troubled firm?"

Of course, they are not. Every company has expectations for a position that may differ slightly from another company or industry—and the position title is the same.

Therefore, it is important for you to truly understand the goals and accountabilities for each position when you interview.

As you interview, you are measuring the company, the hiring manager and the position in real time. Once both of you have completed your interview, you probably know your level of interest. This is a great time to tell the hiring manager that you are interested in the position because "I feel… (Give them some solid reasons regarding the job duties, the manager's management style and/or the company's culture)." As you leave (if you are interested in the position), it is a good time to ask, "Is there anything that would prevent you from offering this position to me?" Why do you ask that question? If you are interested in the job, that question will tell you if there is information that you need to explain, either in a different way or in a bit more detail, and satisfy the hiring manager's objection.

You know you just had a great interview when you emerge from the interview sweating and smiling!

Your brain plays games with you sometimes. Once you get 15 to 20 minutes away from the interview, you will begin to remember aspects of the conversation that I refer to as the "Wish I Would

Have Saids." Find a quiet place—restaurant or café where you can order a soda or coffee, a library or park, or even your own car—to sit down and make some notes about your conversation/conversations. This is an important exercise for several reasons.

1. Most people cannot prepare so completely for an interview as to be prepared to give the best example stories for each skill within the context of a new company.

2. If you do not write the stories to focus on, I guarantee that you will remember that you had "Wish I Would Have Saids," but to save your life, you can't remember a single one. If you get a second interview with the company, this new information should be mentioned. It can mean the difference between an offer or not. If there is no second interview, this information may be used for negotiation if a lower-than-expected offer is extended. We will cover that in the salary negotiation step coming up.

3. Finally, do you really want to differentiate yourself from the other candidates? **Sit down and handwrite a personal thank you note to each person who participated in the interview.** Unfortunately, today most candidates forget that common courtesy. People

remember when you take this extra step. Many candidates question whether they should simply send a thank you note via email. Certainly a good question, however a busy manager may not receive your email because of the company spam filter or they may ignore it in the mass of emails they are dealing with. They will open a card.

Now let's discuss how to impress with your references.

A very strong reference can make the difference between receiving an offer that you will absolutely accept and not receiving an offer.

Enlightened companies and hiring managers understand the importance of an effective reference check.

This television interview discusses reference checking—https://www.youtube.com/watch?v=diMU8yjuUeI

Don't let people tell you that reference checking is dead. Too many times I've heard managers say the reference check is a waste of time. Legally, it may be regaining importance as the final due diligence before hiring a candidate. Therefore, it is important to be able to contact several people who can discuss you as an employee or different skills you have demonstrated. Companies usually require three professional references who can intelligently discuss your professional abilities. If you are a college recruit and have not worked part-time during college, they may take references from professors or a personal reference from someone who has known you for a long time.

I once interviewed a female programmer/analyst. Her responses demonstrated that she knew what she was doing professionally. She offered me several references. So, I called her most recent reference, a female manager, and mentioned that the candidate had given me her name as a reference. When the manager burst out laughing, I thought, "That's not a good sign!"

The manager asked me if I had met the candidate in person. I replied that I had. She said, "You probably noticed that she was gorgeous." I replied that I did. The manager said she had hired the candidate. She was very talented; however, after working there for a short period of time, she began to date one of her coworkers. After an intimate relationship that lasted several months, she broke off the relationship—and began dating another co-worker. Evidently, she whispered some of her previous relation's interesting preferences to her new friend.

Shortly after, the manager found the two males fist fighting in the hall over this woman. All three were looking for new jobs after the fight.

Obviously, this was not a person I would introduce to a client. Be sure to check with your references prior to giving their names to a potential employer. If they are excited to be a reference, that's a great sign. If they are reticent, it's best to move on. It is a good idea to coach a reference just prior to the call from either a manager or human resources representative. How do you coach a reference? As an active listener during your interview, you generally can tell if the manager is concerned about your ability to professionally perform one or more of the required duties of a position. Suggest to the reference that they bring up a specific success that you had while working with them to demonstrate that skill. References appreciate this type of guidance. Otherwise, they are trying to remember examples that may be several years or more in the past.

The references that you choose to discuss your abilities should be people who have seen you successfully perform related, required duties while working with them. Therefore, one reference may be able to discuss your management capabilities. Another reference may be able to focus on your technical abilities. (In this case, "technical" means your day-to-day functions, whether you are a nurse, recruiter, CFO, writer, mechanic or software engineer.) The final reference may focus on your strategic abilities (project planning, long-term planning, budgeting, etc.). Management references are best. Sales or sales-support professionals may want to use one or more clients as references. Just be careful if this is a confidential search.

When you forward your references for a position, note where the person may be able to give the best feedback on your abilities. This information will help coach the person conducting the reference check. Obviously, all references need to be able to discuss your fit within their organizations and whether they would hire you again.

Once you reach this point in the series of processes, you are nearing a successful conclusion to your search.

For a list of potential interview questions, see Appendix B beginning on page 323.

Job Search PROCESS Checklist—
Impressive Interviewing

- ✓ Your skills assessment is done; however, it is a dynamic document that may change according to your memory and the jobs you locate.

- ✓ Your base resume is completed. You change your resume to reflect the needs of each company that you either apply to or interview with. Remember to save each resume version with the name of the company and position title.

- ✓ **You continue to network and grow your networking contacts—especially after you have set up interviews.** Keep your networking momentum going!

- ✓ In preparation for each interview (even second interviews with the same company), research the company and review your notes. What challenges can you help it overcome?

- ✓ You have reviewed the different interviewing formats.

- ✓ You have practiced the different interviewing methods to be confident in your responses to different styles of questions. Prepare for the interview by reviewing the list of potential interview questions in Appendix B.

- ✓ You checked to ensure your cell phone is off. It is embarrassing when it rings during an interview. If you answer it, you probably will not receive an offer.

- ✓ Remember to ask the manager about the three month, six month, nine month and twelve month goals early in the conversation.

- ✓ You have developed responses to both your strengths and weaknesses questions.

- ✓ As the interview is coming to completion, you tell the manager that you are interested in the position—and why.

- ✓ Prepare a list of potential references prior to your interview. Some may be former managers. Others may be able to discuss certain technical skills (nursing procedures, sales skills, programming skills, etc.)

- ✓ After your conversation, go somewhere quiet and list your "Wish I Would Have Saids." These are better examples than the ones you used during the interview. You may use these examples in second interviews and salary negotiations.

This is a natural segue into the next step—

STEP 11: "The Art of Salary Negotiation."

I AM A PROFESSIONAL!

I GOT THIS!

RecruiterGuy.com Series

STEP 11

The Professional Art of Salary Negotiation

Congratulations! You have overcome the other challenging aspects of your search to reach the compensation discussion. While some people enjoy negotiating their compensation with a potential new employer, this is generally an uncomfortable area for most people, especially if their jobs did not require negotiating skills. What is your service worth to a new company?

Every company is different, even in the same industry. Many value positions differently. Salary negotiation is also an area where executives have more leverage than most mid-level professional candidates. I include a negotiating script later in this step that may benefit an executive more than a professional, but you may certainly try it at all levels. College recruits usually have little opportunity to negotiate beyond some money for relocation expenses.

Regarding college recruits, once I extended an offer to a married college recruit. She was an outstanding MIS grad from a major university. When I called to extend her the offer, I could tell she was a little excited, despite the fact that she was trying to be cool. Later, she told me her husband was standing next to her—and both were jumping up and down! Tough to be cool when you are that excited. She almost pulled it off. Oh…and she accepted!

By the way, keep networking throughout your salary-negotiation process.

Employee 5.0, your job is to continue networking even after your start with a new company. Until both sides are happy with your offer, it is not done. One or the other side may step away from the negotiations. Therefore, keep networking until you start your first day. At this point you are saying, "I should keep networking after we negotiated an offer that I accepted?" Yes. You cannot control the economy nor terrorist attacks nor other potential impacts on a company. I have had candidates call me the day they were supposed to start with a new company, only to discover the company suffered a downturn and could not hire them on their start date. Generally, that does not happen at the executive level because of potential lawsuits, but I have seen it happen several times at mid-level and technical positions.

In the first step, I covered taking stock of your skills. Later, we discussed the importance of including your impacts in your resume and interview. Some people told me that "I just did my job. I don't have any impacts."

If you "just did your job," of course you made impacts! Companies do not hire people to take up space and salaries/benefits. One hopes you did the best job you could. For instance, let's say you were a cashier. When you are finished with your shift, does your cash drawer balance every time? Isn't that a positive, measurable impact? You can talk about being detail-oriented and dependable, qualities that every hiring manager seeks. Wouldn't it be cool to be able to say that "my cash drawer balanced every day for the past four years?"

Even some overly modest C-level executive candidates have made that comment to me about "just doing my job" during the distress immediately following a reduction in force. They should discuss their successful strategic decisions, how their cost-cutting suggestions added profits to the bottom line, how their inspired leadership led to an engaged workforce. One place to look for your impacts is your old annual or board reviews.

Create paper copies to store in your home files. If you wait until you depart a company to look at your reviews, it is too late. They just deleted you from their system.

Therefore, it doesn't matter whether you are an executive or a cashier. The complexity of the work is the difference between the jobs. Both levels of work are important to the successful company.

"When do you feel that salary negotiation begins?" is a question that I ask during my salary negotiation presentation to candidates. My feeling is that salary negotiation begins when the company decides to open a position and gives compensation for that position a budget number. The company now has a level of compensation that demonstrates how it values the position. It is a *range* they are willing to pay for that work.

This is a good time to remind you that a company places a certain value on a position. You may feel you may be worth more or need more but to that company the position is worth only what they budgeted. Many times, a person has shared with me that their spouse wanted to be a stay-at-home parent, and therefore they "needed" more money. Your financial situation is not the company's issue. It is yours.

Don't begin that conversation with a representative of the company or your recruiter. That discussion raises questions on your judgment. Do not attempt to present your problems as their problems.

Some companies will require a candidate to put compensation requirements in a cover letter when a resume is submitted. This is one of their screens. I ask every candidate about salary requirements to see whether I feel their expectations are "reasonable." After so many years in the recruitment industry, I generally have a pretty good feel for current salary ranges for most positions. In this step, you will learn how to handle those compensation/salary requests.

Let's get back to discussing compensation conversations. As a candidate, it is important to understand the value that a company puts on a job. If you were contributing at a high level within a large company, you may be surprised how the value may change in a smaller company. In some smaller companies, your value may be substantially higher. Whereas in another company, they may feel that you were over-compensated. You may think it's a minefield out there; however, there are ways to navigate/manage through it.

Now would be a good time to read Alina Tugend's column in the *New York Times—Job Hunting's Delicate Dance* where we discuss salary negotiations: http://www.nytimes.com/2012/07/28/your-money/job-huntings-delicate-dance-shortcuts.html

Many companies do not understand that "recruiting is sales." You can use that to your advantage. Most recruiters do not want to waste their time. If they ask you what you were making at a previous job, respond by asking "What is the compensation/salary/hourly range for this position?"

Many times, their response will save everyone time. Simply put, if the company does not value the work produced by this position, you either have a wonderful opportunity to prove them wrong or you may have a situation that will provide you with many frustrating days if your work is not valued.

I once received a call from a recruiting firm asking if I would be interested in a contract recruiting consulting assignment in Des Moines. I said, "Sure." Then I asked the hourly rate the client was willing to pay. She replied, "$17.50 per hour." I chuckled and told her I hadn't worked for so little since the 1970s. Obviously, they did not value talent acquisition very highly. If you pay for a clerk, that's probably what you'll get.

Hourly workers have less room for negotiation than professional workers. If you are applying for a union position, the company may pay you more for the work than the union contract. However, they may also just use the union contract as their excuse to pay that amount. If they feel you have more promise than most candidates, they will pay more.

A way for anyone to begin a salary negotiation is to ask, "Is there any flexibility in the offer?" They may say, "Why do you ask?" If they do, they have cracked open the door for a discussion to increase the offer. Then you may mention some of your "Wish I Would Have Said" comments from your review of the interview. Ask if they might be willing to increase the offer base or give a signing bonus. Sometimes companies are willing to give an extra week of vacation or increase the relocation package if that is required. Don't expect a large increase in your base compensation. They usually have extended an offer that is within a range in their budget or comparable to others in similar positions in their company.

If the person who is extending the offer says it is their final offer, you have a decision to make. As the result of your interviews with them, do you feel they are going to promote you if you do a great job and make positive measurable impacts? If the answer is yes and the offer is close to your requirements, then you may decide to accept.

If the answer to that question is no, then you should think hard about declining, but do so in a positive manner and ask that they get back to you if another position opens where you may be able to make impacts. As the RecruiterGuy, I have had several experiences where the company realized that a professional turned out to be the right one, realized the offer was too low and came back with a higher compensation package. That doesn't happen often, but it does happen.

Negotiation is an art, not a science. Most importantly, remember not to take the negotiations personally. While I realize that it is personal to you and your family, remember that essentially you are "selling" your services to the new company; therefore, this is a business sales situation and objectivity is important. Don't be afraid to walk away from an offer that is too low. It obviously is the wrong position for you. We don't work these long hours just to be frustrated in our job. Again, if they do not value the position highly enough to pay your worth, you will be frustrated almost daily.

Please do not fall into the trap of asking "for a week to think about an offer" that you know you are going to accept. What do you gain by doing that? What do you lose? They may feel you will accept but keep looking. That's not a positive way to begin a working relationship. On the other hand, what happens when you accept that same offer immediately? You send a message to your future manager and company that you are excited about working with them. Isn't that the way to begin your professional relationship?

Now I am going to touch on a sensitive subject. Even if you are religiously devout, it is best if you do not say that you are going to "pray on this offer." If that is the case, hopefully you have been praying through the whole process. God probably has already indicated whether it is right for you. You just need to listen. The reason I mention this topic is that I have received that response more than you would believe over the years. If you insist on responding in that fashion, the result may be that the company will find a way to rescind the offer because you concerned them that you may spend time proselytizing during work hours, not working; or worse yet, simply cannot decide. Just say, "I'm excited about your offer. May I get back to you tomorrow or Wednesday?" Keep it simple.

Once you accept the offer, honor your commitment. When an offer is accepted, a company stops all recruiting on that position. The manager is excited that you accepted and has probably already penciled you into some projects or scheduled you to work. If you change your mind, they must begin recruiting from the beginning, and that may put the manager months behind. Obviously, you should never expect to work with them in the future because your integrity is now called into question.

If you are employed, it is best to give two weeks' notice. It is the expectation of your current employer. You never want to burn bridges.

The Salary-Negotiation Script

Before I go through the salary-negotiation script with you, understand that while it has been proven effective, when dealing with people and their emotions, nothing works 100 percent of the time. Pay attention not only to what the other person says but how they say it. If you sense they are not receiving it well, you may need to change your direction, or decide that you may not want to work with them. Too often, the human resources representative is young and inexperienced and may be defensive. The seasoned HR executive generally will be fine.

If you are an executive, you may be negotiating with either the board of directors or the executive management team. They understand how to negotiate and probably will be a little disappointed if you don't try to negotiate a better package.

One of the CEOs that I work with often once commented to me after a Vice President of Sales accepted their offer. "I wish they had negotiated a little tougher. They will need to do so for our benefit. It would have been nice to see how they performed."

Review the example of the executive in the book's introduction who used this script to secure a much larger offer than he expected.

Now we can discuss the script.

After the company budgets for the position, what is the next step in the salary-negotiation process? Generally, someone representing the company will call you for an initial phone screen and level of interest measurement. They usually will ask your current compensation or your desired level of compensation. It is best to sidestep this question by asking, "What is the range on this position?" If it is too low, you may just thank them for their interest and mention that if another position opens at a higher level, "Please contact me." There have been times when my clients felt this one professional needed to be hired. They closed the current employee requisition. Then they approved a new requisition at a higher level to justify the level of compensation.

If they pressure you for a number, just respond that every company is different, and every job has different responsibilities, therefore, "Let's not get the cart ahead of the horse. Let's determine if I have the required skills to make positive impacts and if I fit your culture. Once we have those issues settled, I am certain we can reach an agreement on a fair level of compensation." Remember, you may be measured during this time on your ability to negotiate for the company.

Companies operate in different ways during the process. Some may require executive-level candidates to complete an application. Others may not. If they require you to complete an application, you are facing the next opportunity for the company to find your compensation requirements. Most applications have a space titled "Salary Requirement."

How do you handle the "Salary Requirement" space on an application? Easy. Simply write or type "Open." It is easy to remember, hard to misspell and does not lock you into a number. Do not write "Negotiable" for a couple of reasons. I have seen "negotiable" misspelled every conceivable way (I think) over the years.

"Negotiable" usually does not fit the space well, which forces you to shorten it to "Neg" or "Negot." (The company doesn't want you writing REALLY BIG numbers in that space!)

In today's world, you may be required to complete an online application. In those applications, they will not accept letters that spell "Open". Instead, they will accept numbers only. It is the company's way to force you to "spill the beans." The RecruiterGuy "hack" to this problem is to write "1". When the question is asked, "Why did you write 1 for salary requirement?" Your response is, "It showed up as '1'? Is something wrong with your software?" Then revert to "cart before the horse."

So much of an executive's compensation is based on stock, bonuses, and other incentives that while salary is important, it is only part of an entire package. Therefore, executives need to consider the whole package instead of total focus on salary.

If you decide to write a salary number in the space, only one good thing can happen, and two bad things can happen—not good odds.

The only possible good thing that can happen is for the manager to complete the interview and say to you, "Margaret (or Mason), wow this must be a meeting of the minds; $101,256 is *exactly* what we were going to offer you!"

If people can't successfully guess the right number between 1 and 10, how do you expect them or you to guess exactly the right number, especially when we're talking five-, six- or seven-figure incomes?

What are the two bad things that can happen? One is that you may overshoot what they are willing or able to pay for a base, therefore eliminating yourself from the competition. They may have been willing to give you a competitive base and a piece of the company if you were the right level professional and able to create the right results. If your research showed they had a tremendous potential like Google in their early years, you may have been willing to accept that challenge.

The other bad thing that could happen is that they may have been willing to give you a larger package than you wrote in "Salary Requirement." Because you wrote a lower number, they want to make you happy and that could be your offer. That gives you a weak negotiating stance because it's the number you gave them.

Back in the 1980s, I was working with a technology professional coming out of the military.

He was a sharp guy. Because he was in the military, his salary was a little lower than normal—in the low $30,000s. During our conversations, we agreed that he would allow me to conduct his salary negotiations. I then proceeded to discuss this salary-negotiation education with him. Prior to his interview, I negotiated a salary of $42,000 with the manager should he pass his interview and technical skills. During his interview, he completed the application.

In "Salary Requirement" he wrote "$35,000" as his expectation. Guess what? The manager wanted to make him happy and she saved her budget $7,000 in the first year alone. It took him four years to get to the level I negotiated for him prior to his interview. Of course, I could not tell him about his miscue.

The application also has another area where the company may qualify your compensation—your job history. In most applications, they ask for your starting and ending compensation or salary. When completing this area, place an * in those spaces.

At the bottom of the page, write "* Will be willing to discuss at the appropriate time during the interview." Actually, you never really want to discuss these numbers because it is your private financial information.

The one field where you may be required to give this information is sales. Unfortunately, some sales professionals have a history of inflating their numbers, especially commissions. Be prepared to show management your W-2 from the previous year.

Of course, the same engineers developed the Salary Requirement box and the current and last salary in your job history. If they are the same engineers, everything is good! Simply try the $0 or the $1 in those boxes. When asked about the number, just ask, "Is that what it says? Is your system broken?"

Once you have completed your application and handed it in, the human resource professional will generally glance through it to ensure you have filled all open spaces. When they see that you wrote "open" in the "Salary Requirement" space, they usually ask you what "open" means. Here is your response (understand that I know you will change this script to better fit your personality or the position, but keep all the elements):

"Until I meet with the manager or board and truly know:

- ✓ what the job entails;

- ✓ what you expect from me;

- ✓ what positive, measurable impacts I can make;

- ✓ and where I can grow within the company over the next five years;

- ✓ I cannot make an intelligent assessment on a fair level of compensation. Let's move on with the interview so we can get those questions answered."

Isn't that statement correct? Without that information and understanding of the challenges and potential impacts, how do you assign a compensation number to a position? Additionally, it is important for you to get a sense for how the company values this position.

This script also gives both you and the manager a platform for your interview if the manager asks you what "open" means. Even if they don't hear your script, you can use it as a base of the conversation.

During your interview, it is important to get agreement on where they feel you may be able to make measurable impacts. Make note of these on a separate page in your notepad.

Once your interview is over, the manager or board member may say, "Now you know what the job entails, what we expect from you, where you may be able to make impacts and where you may be able to grow within the next five years. What is your assessment of a fair level of compensation?"

If you are truly interested in the position, your response should follow these lines: "I am very interested in your position because of what the job entails (mention 2 or 3 requirements about what the job entails that are attractive to you) and what you expect from me (mention 2 or 3 areas that excite you). Can we chat briefly about the potential impacts I can make?" Here, go over your list of agreed impacts, reinforcing that you are an impact performer. Finally, discuss the positive side of the potential future growth.

Then say, "As the result of my interview(s) you have a much better feel where I fit into your corporate compensation structure than I will ever have. I am very interested in this position. You know your salary structure. It is not good for me to be paid too high nor it is good to be paid too low compared to my peers. Please make me the best offer that you can, and I will sincerely consider it."

This gives you a salary-negotiation strategy. The first party that puts a number on the table loses negotiation leverage.

This script enables you to push salary negotiation where it belongs—when both parties indicate an interest in each other.

As I mentioned in Step 6 on "Impressive Interviewing," once you get 15 to 20 minutes from your interview, sit down in a quiet place and jot down your "Wish I Would Have Saids." These are the better examples of your experience and past impacts that you should have used during the interview. They may be introduced in your salary negotiation if an offer is extended.

After a successful interview where both sides indicate interest in each other, you may receive a call to return so they can extend you an offer in person. Or, they may choose to call you to extend an offer over the phone. Different companies handle offers in different ways. If a third-party recruiter is involved, the recruiter strongly prefers to extend the offer. Sometimes, a human resource professional will extend the offer. In other companies, the hiring manager makes the call to extend an offer.

Many times, companies will extend a contingent offer prior to completing their due diligence of reference checking and drug test results. The offer is contingent upon the successful completion of those items. Executives may need to go through a credit check, particularly if they handle or have access to corporate finances.

Up until now, have we negotiated a salary? No. We've just negotiated whether you would tell them your salary requirements and created a foundation for your interview.

When you receive your offer, if you are going to try to negotiate a higher base, bonus, options, higher relocation benefits, etc., now is the time to ask, "Do you have any flexibility in your offer?" There will probably be one of two answers.

They may say something along the lines of, "You asked us to give you our best offer. This is it." Now you have a decision to make. Is this the right position and right company for me?

As we covered earlier, however, they may say, "Why do you ask?" If they ask that question, the door is cracked open for you to reply, "I am very interested in this position and working with you (or the manager or board). I was hoping for a larger package. Additionally, while I was reviewing our conversation, there were a few examples that better demonstrate the impacts I could make here. Could we spend a few minutes chatting about them?"

If you are asking for additional compensation, remember it is a good idea to give the company additional information on which to base their decision. Otherwise, it is very easy for them to say that their compensation decision was based on the information you gave them.

Companies typically will not increase the base compensation offer by a large percentage because they do not want to negatively impact their compensation ranges. They do have other ways to increase your compensation for this year, particularly if you must accept a cut in your base.

The first way a company may supplement your base income is to offer a signing bonus. This allows you to earn the same or more than you did at your last job without impacting their base compensation. Next budget year, they can decide to raise the compensation bands or give you a promotion (if deserved). Generally, the signing bonus is given on your first day. Some companies will hold all or a portion of your bonus until you work past the probationary period.

Another way that companies can add income is by adding a week or so of paid vacation to your package. This is a particularly attractive alternative for people who like to travel or treasure their days off. The key is to take the time off.

Some companies will offer quarterly and annual bonuses. When I worked for a startup as a manager, I was constantly amazed when I was paid a bonus and the company was not showing a profit; however, I did accept the check. These bonuses generally are based on the individual and the company hitting certain measurable targets.

After the Alternative Minimum Tax (AMT) issues where people lost their homes, stock options lost much of their popularity. Now, because Congress never bothered to index AMT to inflation in 1969 until 2013, it is beginning to impact middle income families. Congress will neither repeal nor change the law. So, if a company offers you stock options and it appears that the company is ready to grow quickly, talk to your tax accountant about protecting yourself and then decide whether or how to accept them.

During 1969, Congress passed the Alternative Minimum Tax law because there was a tax loophole being used by wealthy individuals and corporations to avoid paying income taxes. In 1970, only approximately 20,000 high worth individuals were impacted by that tax.[2] Since the tax was not indexed to inflation, by 2012 approximately 4 million Americans were impacted. In 2013, Congress

---

[2] https://www.learnvest.com/knowledge-center/the-amt-is-not-the-same-thing-as-the-atm/2/

finally indexed AMT to inflation. How may this law impact you as a Middle-Class employee? If you receive Incentive Stock Options as part of your compensation, the difference between the purchase price and the grant price is subject to AMT (but not to income taxes). What may the impact be?

During the Dot.com years, many employees were offered lower compensation and many stock options. This was a vehicle to wealth if everything worked as planned. Well, you know Murphy and His Law. When the recession hit, many people were taxed in one year based on the difference in their purchase rice and the grant price (worth) of their stock options. Only to find the worth of their stock dropped early the next year below their purchase price. Therefore, they could not sell enough stock to cover their Alternative Minimum Tax for the previous year. Many Americans lost their homes as a result.

When you negotiate your compensation, think of your negotiation as a total package. Therefore, once you negotiate your package, and the company accepts your request, it is time to accept your offer. It you try to negotiate more after the company gives what you ask, how do you think they will feel?

Recently my client, whose headquarters was overseas, extended an offer to a young man a year out of college. He was working for a Big 4 Accounting firm. He was married in August. By October, his wife wondered why they were married—he was away so much. By the time we interviewed after Thanksgiving, he was ready to change companies.

I interviewed him and forwarded the phone screen to my client, recommending they schedule an onsite interview. After the interview, the hiring manager decided to offer him the accounting position. The Human Resource Manager extended the offer. He negotiated a 10% increase in his base salary. She needed to forward the new offer overseas (and overnight) for corporate approval.

The new offer was approved and she extended the offer. To her dismay, he then mentioned that he and his wife liked to travel. "Could I get an extra week's vacation?" That is when she called me. I told her I would chat with him.

At the beginning of my call, I told him that the HR Manager and I were in daily contact. "Congratulations on receiving a very attractive offer; and negotiating a higher salary successfully. The good news is that since travel is so important to you, you will be able to continue traveling as much as before." He responded with a "Thanks…Pause…Why?"

"She gave me the authority to rescind your offer. "

"What? I want the offer!"

"Great! You have 10 seconds to accept it or I will rescind it. It appears that you are more interested in this offer for you than both you and the company."

"I didn't mean that! I accept!"

"Congratulations! Will you start in two weeks?" He committed to starting in two weeks. Then he asked if he could talk with the HR Manager. I told him that he could but to give me thirty minutes to give her the great news about his acceptance. He spoke with her and took his signed offer letter to her that day.

A ten percent increase over an original offer does not happen very often. If you receive that much of an increase, it is best to accept and start. If the offer is less than you were making the year before, ask if the company can pay you a sign on bonus to help make you whole this year. Then they can budget the increase for you in the next budget—if you deserve the raise.

Depending on your position, some companies will offer a car. Again, just understand the potential tax impact. The Internal Revenue Service considers the lease value as income.

Finally, if moving is required, the relocation package may be an area that can have a positive impact on your decision. Few companies are willing to buy houses these days, at least at a price that people are willing to accept. Many people are not able to sell their house at the house's current appraised value. So, there's a loss before you move. You may be able to compensate for this loss in other areas of your relocation package. Possibly have the company pack and move you instead of just moving you. **Also remember that not all expenses are deductible for income tax purposes. You may negotiate that the company increase your relocation package to cover the difference in the loss from income taxes.**

Once we were packed by a moving company. I made the bad mistake of leaving my suitcase with my clothes for the trip and my next day at the office in my bathtub. I told three people not to pack it. When someone called me out to our garage to ask if we were taking or leaving something, my suitcase must have fit perfectly in a box. When I returned, the suitcase was packed—and probably already on the truck. Next time, anything that I don't want packed will be in my rental car before they arrive. I had to buy clothes, toiletries and an inexpensive duffle to get through the next two days.

If you are moving middle school or high school-age children, ask the new company if the children can accompany you on your first house-hunting trip. The children may yell and scream regarding the move, but they are more flexible than you give them credit. They just want some say in their move; therefore, set up meetings with principals or curriculum specialists and coaches, drama teachers, music teachers, (any other special-interest professionals), prior to your house-hunting trip. In your request for the meeting, coach the individual to address the children, not you. Set these meetings to give them a choice of school districts if you can. Then look for housing in the school district the children select.

Your move will be easier if your children are also "recruited" to the new area.

If your spouse works and will need to find a job in the new area, ask for job-search help for your spouse. It can be formal or informal help. Depending on your spouse, networking may be difficult in a new area. Any introductions your company can make will certainly help with acceptance of the move.

During the same move that I described above, my wife interviewed at two hospitals in the new city during our house-hunting trip. It gave her a sense for the area and her potential employment opportunities. After returning to Maryland, she received an offer from one of those hospitals. Her acceptance of that offer made her feel better about our move.

Therefore, your salary negotiations may include the request for benefits that you have not considered.

Caution: if you are really interested in this job, pick and choose the benefits or increases that you need. Do not just run the checklist of all of them at the same time.

If the company gets the sense you are just interested in taking an offer to your current company to receive a counter offer, do not be surprised if they rescind theirs. As a professional recruiter, it is easy to tell when a candidate is shopping to receive a counter offer from their current firm. All of a sudden, they begin to make excuses to avoid making commitments to start—or they stop returning calls.

What a nice segue to the next step, "Resignation and the Temptation of the Counter Offer."

First, let's go through our checklist for the salary-negotiation process for people who are truly interested in the position.

Job-Search PROCESS Checklist—
Art of Salary Negotiation

- ✓ You continue to network until your first day on the new job. There is no need to tell the people with whom you are networking that you expect an offer. Networking remains the same. Continue to interview. You never know if an offer will be rescinded because of a sudden company downturn or the new company suddenly finds a better qualified candidate than you. These new people become part of your larger network once you start any new position. **Employee 5.0, the first months are just a pause in your networking as you learn your new position—inside or outside your current company.**

- ✓ You review your list of "Wish I Would Have Saids" that you created after your interviews.

- ✓ When an offer is extended, the first thing you should do is tell them you are interested in the job and in working with them. Then you may either accept their offer if you are happy with it or ask if they have some flexibility.

- ✓ If they have some flexibility, ask if you can discuss your new information (Wish I Would Have Saids) that may impact their offer.

- ✓ Assure them that you are very interested in their position and working with them.

- ✓ It is important to negotiate your offer with them in a positive fashion. Do not take these negotiations personally.

- ✓ Discuss various options with them regarding increased base compensation, signing bonus, quarterly and annual bonuses, stock or stock options, increased vacation time, relocation benefits, education benefits, relocation benefits (if appropriate). Keep in mind benefits that some companies have that differentiate themselves from other companies.

- ✓ When you are happy with your negotiations, be prepared to accept their final offer immediately and commit to an agreed start date. I hope the information presented here helps you in your negotiations!

Salary negotiation TV interview where we discuss counter offers—https://www.youtube.com/watch?v=y4qJWd7-bt8

Remain positive!

People do what you expect them to do. Good luck!

I AM A PROFESSIONAL.

I GOT THIS!

RecruiterGuy.com Series

STEP 12

Resignation and the Temptation of the Counter Offer

In STEP 1, "Our First Steps Together," I discussed how our society values stability over change. Additionally, most people are uncomfortable with conflict; therefore, resigning from your current position can be very stressful. Few people find it easy to resign and really don't know how to end that professional relationship.

It is important to end your tenure at a company in a positive way. Employees at your company remember how you transitioned work prior to your departure. Remember, managers also change jobs. You never know if you will see one later in a new company.

Your resignation is a process—and some of you probably thought it was simply, "I quit."

The best way to resign is to write a resignation letter. It needs to be simple, positive and clear. It is also a way for you to avoid the initial potential conflict. Generally, managers will absorb the fact that you are resigning before coming to you to ask questions about your resignation.

This is a sample resignation letter:

Date

Dear *Manager* (obviously, use their name):

I want to thank you for the time that I have spent working with you. This has been a time of personal and professional growth for me. *Company Name* (your current employer) is a great company; however, I have received and accepted an offer to work with another great company. This new position helps me further my professional goals, and I am looking forward to starting with them on (start date).

My last day with *Company Name* will be Friday, Month Day (two-weeks' notice). During the next two weeks, I will transition any uncompleted work to co-workers.

The decision to leave is a final decision for me. I have no interest in receiving a counter offer.

Sincerely,
(your signature)
John Doe

As you can see, the information is concise and positive. There is no need to share the name of your new employer.

When asked why you are leaving, simply say the new position is with a company that will give you the opportunity to grow and make new impacts—and that you are really looking forward to working with the new company.

Your manager needs to know that you are happy with your decision to leave and will not consider a counter offer. Tell your manager if he/she has any transitional questions after your departure that you are willing to answer any of those questions.

If the manager pushes you to stay longer than two weeks to transition your work, remember **any additional time in the position may be very painful when they pressure you to accept a counter offer—and they will pressure you almost daily.** I've worked with candidates who called me in their third week. They were complaining to me that it was not about transitioning work. The company was pressuring them to stay. I suggested that the next day they announce, "The transition is completed, so I am leaving at noon to start with my new company. It has been a pleasure working with you! Thank you!"

Employee 5.0

As your performance was measured during your tenure with that company, your performance as you depart will be measured and remembered. Make it as positive a memory as you can.

Emotions run high during the time when you resign. So, there is no surprise when someone tells me they have decided to accept a counter offer within their own company.

Prior to accepting a counter offer, you should attempt to make it a rational decision rather than an emotional decision. Consider that recruiting industry newsletters like the *Fordyce Letter* and online recruiting sites such as https://www.ere.net/ track the percentages of people who accept counter offers and are still with their company six months to a year later.

An amazing 87 percent of all people who accept a counter offer leave their current company within a year after accepting the counter offer to stay.

Think about that for a minute. Las Vegas was built, and all that electricity is paid for by people taking risks when the odds are against them; therefore, of every 1,000 who accepted counter offers, 130 people remain at their company a year later, while 870 of them have left (some of those not by their choice), usually within six months.

The 870 people who left must experience the stress of another job search—and usually have one fewer option since they have broken that trust. Because they were successful enough to receive an offer this time, they should be confident enough to succeed again. But there is no reason to believe the original position is still open—or if the company even would consider them as a candidate again. The original trust has now been broken by acceptance of the counter offer.

Employee 5.0 is focused on their career. Their decision to move on is generally a rational growth decision, not one that was made during an emotional state. Therefore, once they make their decision to leave—and then, accept a new position, the decision is final.

I worked with a candidate who was interested in a management position within a consulting company in the top-secret world. My client was a small boutique consulting company within that world that had a great reputation with its clients. As a result, they were beginning to grow and needed to bring in a technically talented manager to help that growth succeed and continue to grow.

The candidate sailed through the interviews successfully. He had the perfect credentials for my client and the right attitude and skills to manage a small team. As the result of his interviews, the candidate received an offer from my client. When he resigned, his current company offered him a counter offer that matched his newly offered compensation from my client. More important, they offered him the opportunity to lead a team. Since he viewed himself as a loyal employee and his company appeared to match my client's offer, he accepted his company's counter offer.

My client was obviously very disappointed on several levels:

1 *They thought their search for a new manager was over and that he would soon start.*

2 *Once they extended his offer and he accepted, they assumed their search was over and notified other candidates.*

3 *Now they were going to have to begin from scratch to search for a new qualified candidate within a very small community of potential candidates.*

4 *He had broken the trust and the commitment that he made to my client.*

You can probably understand why my client did not want to hear his name later.

And later did come… After he accepted the counter offer, his manager told him that they would begin to expand in several months and that is when he would get the team to manage. As soon as his company heard that a new manager began at my client's company three months later, they told him that they were slowing down their expansion and he would not have a team to manage for the foreseeable future.

Of course, he did still have the extra compensation, but the reason he was looking initially was not money, it was the additional challenge of managing a team. Now he was unhappy again—and his own company broke that trust, again. He immediately called me as soon as his manager gave him that news. "Was the position still available?" I told him that my client just had someone start in the position the day before.

Now he realized that his company had betrayed him and was more disappointed than before he began his first search. My client was not interested in hearing he was available because they felt he broke his commitment to them. He found another position a short time later and left his company.

Why do managers and companies extend counter offers?

There are many reasons:

- ✓ They really need a person to fill that role, and the current person did so nicely (and sometimes below market value, particularly if they have been a long-term employee).

- ✓ They also recognize no other current employee can fill that role.

- ✓ They suddenly recognize the value that person brings, particularly the knowledge of the position and potential competitive intelligence that person will take with them.

- ✓ The manager recognizes he or she will now need to conduct a search for a new employee and spend the time and money to train them.

- ✓ If they leave, someone else will need to perform those tasks until the position is filled by a new person and they are trained.

- ✓ Some people are poor managers. They may have already lost members of their team and are afraid how this next departure will impact their future as a manager.

- ✓ They are also afraid that this departure, particularly if the person is well-liked, may trigger more employees to look for and find new positions.

- ✓ They are afraid of the impact of the employee's departure on morale.

- ✓ They are afraid of the impact of hiring someone new to their compensation structure, particularly if the current employee discovered the compensation was under market value.

- ✓ They may decide they do not want to compete against you at another company.

Most of the time, concerns revolve around themselves and not their employee. These managers are struggling to maintain their grip on a person who stated they are leaving. Suddenly, an employee who was not so important has become a very important person (for a while).

Those are some of the reasons and fears of the manager and of the company.

So why should an employee be wary of the counter offer?

1. Now your manager and company know you are unhappy there. So, a certain level of trust has been broken within your own company.

2. What are your most important assets to your company now that they know you want to leave? Your knowledge of your position, processes, systems, people, etc. Some of this knowledge will not be replaced for a long time.

3. If they offer you more money during the counter offer, are you setting yourself up to lose next year's raise?

4. Why are you suddenly worth more today—after your resignation—than you were worth yesterday? Many people become upset when they consider this aspect. If a person uses an offer to leverage a counter offer for more pay, companies will probably view that ploy as blackmail. It may work once. Then the company will factor the blackmail in for future "raises."

5 Is there a possibility your company will conduct a brain drain on you after you accept a counter offer? (They know the statistics demonstrate that you will leave within a year as well!) Will they get the information they need from you and then replace you through a reorganization once a new person is up to speed?

6 Remember the premise of behavioral interviewing? Once the manager feels that you are locked in, do you really believe things will change? Probably not!

7 Do you really believe them when they say they are happy you decided to stay? Are they happy for you, or happy for themselves? Now, they have Old Reliable still in the seat and don't have to spend time and money to recruit a replacement.

8 Remember the odds are against success at your company after you resign from that company. They just want someone to do the job until they decide how to "protect themselves," (with a new person ready to assume your responsibilities).

While I preach a good game on counter offers, it took two bad experiences for me to be convinced that accepting a counter offer is unwise.

Both times, I left within six months of the counter offer—the second time I was a successful recruiter and certainly should have known better.

I was a senior recruiter working with a noted contingent recruiting firm with offices in Washington, D.C., and New York City. As I experienced success in the contingency world, I decided that I wanted to mentor and train my own team. There were some things I wanted to do differently than my manager.

After discussions with my manager/partner broke down, I discussed my candidacy with another firm in Maryland a little closer to my home. They made me an offer immediately. I accepted.

When I went back to my manager/partner and resigned, he was dumbfounded. He went on a full-court press to get me to stay, including putting me on a shuttle flight to New York City to visit with his partners. His partners wined and dined me and assured me that we would come to an agreement and I would be able to develop my own team. I returned that evening full of promise and decided to stay there. The other firm was very disappointed that I changed my mind.

Over the next couple of months, I focused primarily on my recruitment fee production while looking for the right talent to recruit. About the time I found someone to hire, the partner had hired someone else to grow his consulting business and told me that it was up to the new manager. The new manager told me that he wanted to go in another direction (consulting). The trust was broken. I left two weeks later.

I am still friendly with my manager/partner there. He acknowledged that he made a bad decision—and so did I. Once I decided to leave the first time, I should have left.

When you resign, what should you expect to hear from your company if they are going to extend a counter offer? Many times, I list these statements for the candidates and ask them to tell me how many they hear. While this is an important time for the departing employee, companies are amazingly consistent in what they say to the person who wants to leave.

1. "I am shocked that you want to leave. I thought you were happy. As a matter of fact, tomorrow we were going to discuss a (promotion, raise, new project, etc.) with you." (Call me a cynic, but the supposed timing is an amazing coincidence, wouldn't you agree?)

2. "You are a very valuable employee. We need to see what we can do to encourage you to stay."

3. "I am happy that you came to me because I planned to chat with you about moving to another organization in our company (that was nixed in previous conversations weeks before)."

4. "I am very disappointed that you chose such a busy time to leave our organization. Can't you see the impact your departure will have on everyone else?" (I love that one. The manager is trying to put a guilt trip on you.)

5. "Your manager just came to me to discuss your resignation. I asked if I could talk with you. You are a key person in our growth plans. I am sorry we haven't shared this with you sooner. Let's sit down and discuss the needed changes…" (Generally, an executive speaking.)

6. "What will it take for you to stay?" (At least that one is up front in its intent!)

7. "As you know, we rarely give counter offers here, but you are such a key person, we will

make an exception. What do you want to stay?"

8 "Thank you for coming to me and discussing needed changes. Would you like to lead those changes?" (If you accept the counter offer, the desire to make immediate changes in the organization dissolves shortly after you accept.) Then they will say, "Let's just finish what you are working on first. Then we will discuss the changes." (Note, they won't say "make the changes" again.)

For your own satisfaction, track how many of these statements you hear when you resign.

My client extended an offer to a candidate who accepted the offer. We sat down. I chatted with him about the counter offer experience that I had personally. Then we discussed the statements that he might hear the next day when he resigned. I suggested that he track them and call me at the end of the day and let me know which ones he heard.

Sure enough, I received a call from him early in the evening after they had taken him to dinner (those wily devils!). He was laughing. He thanked me for my counter-offer counseling. They managed to hit seven out of eight statements. That's certainly better than average! He honored his commitment and went to work with my client.

I have another counter offer story. In 1993, we were traveling across the country looking for candidates for a Midwestern city. One candidate I interviewed received an offer. This is his story.

We extended the offer to this candidate and he accepted on the spot.

He was very excited about his offer. On the Wednesday before he was leaving the company, his manager called him in and put him on the spot. He was great at putting employees on guilt trips, and this one worked. On Thursday morning, I received an email from one of the managers I worked with saying that he accepted a counter offer. I asked the manager if he wanted me to try to "save" him. He replied, "Please!"

I called the candidate and asked if we could sit down for a soda on Saturday afternoon when I was back in town. He said, "Sure."

When we sat down in a restaurant, we chatted for almost an hour over the soda (called "Pop" in some regions of the US or "Coke" in Atlanta) discussing what had happened. When he was finished, I asked him if he was happy that he accepted the counter offer. He was undecided. I suggested that in my experience, when I make a decision that feels right, it seems the weight of the world has left my shoulders. I observed that, based on our chat, it appeared that weight was still there. Then I asked him if he would like me to tell him how to resign and still make orientation on Monday. He said, "Sure."

He told me that his manager usually was in on Mondays by 7 a.m. I told him to get there at 6:30 a.m. and empty his cubicle. When 7 a.m. rolled around, go to the manager and say, "Two weeks ago I turned in my notice. Last week you pressured me to stay. I didn't want to stay, but you pressured me, so I accepted your counter offer. After thinking it over during the weekend, I decided to honor my commitment and go to work for my new company. Here are my keys and identification. I need to run to make orientation." Then leave.

He asked me if he could take time to think about it. I said, "Sure, just let me know tomorrow if you want to be in orientation Monday morning so I can send a note to let them know to expect you. As promised, he called me on Sunday and told me he would be in orientation.

He enjoyed the new company so well that he stayed for 20 years. We are still friends.

Employee 5.0

Bottom line—you made a commitment to your new manager. Honor your commitment.

Job Search PROCESS Checklist — Resignation and the Temptation of the Counter Offer

- ✓ Write a simple, positive resignation letter.

- ✓ When asked why you are leaving, simply say the new position is with a company that will give you the opportunity to grow and make new impacts—and that you are really looking forward to working with the new company.

- ✓ Tell your manager that you are not interested and will not consider a counter offer.

- ✓ Assure the manager that you will ensure your work is transitioned to the team.

- ✓ If pushed to remain on the job longer than two weeks, carefully monitor progress on transitioning work. Once the pressure to accept a counter offer is greater than the pressure to transition work, it is time to leave immediately.

- ✓ Read once more the odds against a successful tenure after accepting a counter offer.

- ✓ Understand the reasons why companies suddenly decide to extend a counter offer.

- ✓ Review the reasons why the employee should be wary of the counter offer.

- ✓ Count how many of the counter-offer-related statements you hear from managers and executives once the word gets out that you resigned.

- ✓ Once you accept an offer and give a start date, honor your commitment to start on that date.

- ✓ Employee 5.0 is decisive. Once you decide the time has come to move, the decision is made and the commitment to the new company is honored.

This is a good time to discuss your first few weeks on the new job in **Step 13: "Your First Day on the Job!**

By now, you and your mirror should be on pretty good terms! It is expecting your visits in the morning and evening. This may be a stressful time. In track, races are lost when runners fail to run through the tape. Continue to run through the tape—

I AM A PROFESSIONAL

I GOT THIS!

STEP 13

Your First Day on the Job!

Congratulations! Doesn't it feel good to have finally reached this point? Typically, you are experiencing many feelings now—elation, anticipation, excitement, enthusiasm and yes, even a little fear. As you have experienced, your job search turned out to be an emotional roller coaster ride and you are happy it's over.

As RecruiterGuy, may I suggest that while everything is fresh in your memory, it is time to prepare for your next search? Jot down what actions were successful for you during this search. What would you have done differently? Think of this as your "debriefing." Document your search for your own records while still fresh in your mind. Remember, you never know when you will be looking again. That's the 5.0 Employee mindset.

I totally understand that deep down you are hoping you will remain with this company for the balance of your career; however, the odds today work against that potential conclusion unless you are at the very end of your career.

In today's merger/acquisition world, positions are cut in to take advantage of "synergies gained by the merger." Other old-line companies are on the slippery slope headed to bankruptcy and reductions in force. Even new companies make poor decisions; and go out of business. **These are all reasons to stay on top of Your Career! Become Employee 5.0. It is a mentality that becomes a way of working and living.**

Remember to thank everyone who helped you in your search and let them know where you are now working. Now that you have a business relationship, they may be a good source to contribute to solutions to problems confounding you, and you may be able to return the favor.

Continue to network with people to see how you can help them. Remember your experience as you went through the job-search process. If you receive a call from someone who is attempting to network the way to a new position, take the call. Without spending an inordinate amount of time, use your experience to make suggestions and help them better focus their search. That's how you pay it forward and become a leader. Remember, you now have a huge list of potential people they can use to network. Obviously, not everyone on your list is good for their search, but at least a few of them are. You may make a difference in the person's life.

Understand that some people are users. Remember the opera singer warming up? Me, me, me, me! Spend tiny amounts of time with them instead and focus on people who understand networking is a two-way street.

One hopes you made some new friends during this journey. Nurture those relationships. They need not involve social interaction. They can be a quick phone call or e-mail asking how the person is doing. Keep your information on LinkedIn up to date and check out their activities occasionally. You may be able to answer a quick question for them.

One of the areas that most people can improve is to track their impacts. You can review this information prior to your annual review with your manager or executive board. If you find yourself in another search, this information will be sitting in a file on your personal computer instead of needing to be dredged up. Managers don't always track your impacts well (as you probably discovered prior to your last move). Therefore, it is your responsibility to track them. As you work through your quarterly or annual reviews, it is good to bring impacts up for discussion. This is not bragging. It is reinforcing in your manager's mind the problems that you are helping them solve.

Once I was in an annual review with my manager. The manager did not mention any of my positive, measurable impacts. That individual took offense that I tracked my accomplishments over the past year. The accomplishments were not inconsequential, included working with an in-house developer to create an applicant tracking software for the company using free-ware that was used for 6 years as the company grew from a 500 employee company to a 10,000 employee company. The manager said, "It's always about you!" It was apparent that I was not in their future plans. I returned to my business after their IPO six months later.

Employee 5.0, pay attention to the following guidance. It applies to every new employee. However, Employee 5.0 uses this guidance to create their competitive advantage inside the company.

As you work with your new manager, come to agreement on three month, six month, nine month and twelve month goals for you. This keeps you on track to fulfill the goals for the year. Ask your manager to introduce you to the people who you will need to interface to accomplish the goals.

It is advisable to make this an annual practice with each manager. During your reviews, you can discuss the goals completed. It also is a good platform to use when you need your manager to introduce you to someone new inside the company or to a vendor to meet your goal.

During these discussions, develop agreement on opportunities you see for your group and the company. Keeping your focus on your goals and company goals is the best way to be viewed as a person who makes a difference within the company. Helping your manager accomplish goals while accomplishing your goals is the vehicle to be viewed as a team player. If you build consensus with others in your company, it also is a great way to grow respect.

Once you have some credibility (by meeting your goals) with your manager, your goal-review time is a great time to discuss your future career goals. If your manager has a mentor type of relationship with you, she or he can be a great person to help position you for your next move.

Remember in Step Four, *"Effective Networking to Your Next Position!"* when I said networking can be a simple conversation that can benefit both sides? Doesn't this also work inside companies? You may not call it networking inside your company, but that's what it is.

Effectively networking within your company is a great way to be more effective working with other staff and management. Networking within your company with other managers is a way to move within your company to gain new experience and make new impacts without taking time to look for a new job in another company. This is an effective practice to break down silos within companies. Many larger companies have organizations focused on only one product or line of products/services. Those organizations have their own management team; and many times, do not communicate well with other lines or teams.

Watch this television interview to learn more about your first day on the job - https://www.youtube.com/watch?v=72ewi2FbuIc&feature=youtu.be

Remember the goal of having so much fun at work that at the end of the day you say, "Wow! This was so much fun that I can't believe today is already over—and they are paying me, too!" How do you reach that level of job satisfaction? You reach it by making positive, measurable impacts and having fun. Meet your goals and help others meet theirs.

As you are meeting your goals, look for dirty jobs that others are avoiding. In my experience, these "dirty jobs" have such a reputation of being time traps or are such a pain to do that they develop the reputation of being a monster. These are great places to learn Lean (Agile) process improvement skills or become certified Six Sigma process improvement professional. Then tackle one of those jobs at a time from a Lean (Agile) process-improvement or Six Sigma focus that eliminates waste to practice your new skills.

What you may discover is that your fresh look at the task can help you suggest improvements at the level that other people don't mind doing it; or you eliminated waste and contributed directly to the bottom line. You also may decide to automate it so no one must do it again. You may discover it has outlasted its usefulness. Of course, before discarding information or deleting a task, confirm with your manager that it no longer needs attention.

People who successfully clean up the dirty jobs and make them efficient are the ones who succeed within companies.

Do we need a checklist at the end of this book? This one is easy:

Make IMPACTS and Have fun!

Finally, why not?

I AM A PROFESSIONAL!

I GOT THIS!

And you have proven that you do! Congratulations!

Employee 5.0

APPENDIX A

Resume Action Verbs and Phrases

These verbs and phrases can be used to create more interest in your resume. Once you are interviewing, some of your material on your resume will be the base of your interview. Prepare yourself for your interview by creating true stories that demonstrate the skills in your resume. (See Step 4, page 81.)

These verbs and phrases have been separated by level of position (executive job searches, professional and sales job searches and entry level job searches); but they are by no means mutually exclusive. Feel free to draw from each list as needed.

Obviously, every field has its own jargon, so this list is not totally complete. The purpose is to give you a start that will help you remember more specific action verbs that apply to your experience.

The convention in resume writing is to write your sentences in third person past tense as if you were describing someone else's experience, even your current experience, and then drop the pronouns. You will note that these verbs are written in past tense.

Executive Search Action Verbs

Accelerated
Achieved
Acquired
Added
Administered
Analyzed
Appraised
Assimilated
Assumed
Assured
Augmented
Authored
Awarded
Balanced
Built
Captured
Catapulted
Chaired
Challenged
Championed
Charted
Cleared
Closed
Coached
Collaborated
Communicated
Competed
Compiled
Completed
Composed
Conceived
Conceptualized
Conducted
Consolidated
Consulted
Converted
Coordinated
Counseled
Created
Cut
Defined
Delivered
Deployed
Developed
Devised
Directed
Distinguished
Diversified
Divested
Downsized
Dreamed/Dreamt
Drove
Eliminated

- Engaged
- Engineered
- Enhanced
- Ensured
- Established
- Evaluated
- Exceeded
- Executed
- Expanded
- Experienced
- Finalized
- Financed
- Finessed
- Focused
- Found
- Founded
- Funded
- Generated
- Grasped
- Guided
- Honed
- Identified
- Imagined
- Immersed
- Implemented
- Improved
- Increased
- Indicated
- Initiated
- Instituted
- Integrated
- Interacted
- Interfaced
- Introduced
- Invested
- Launched
- Led
- Leveraged
- Licensed
- Linked
- Loaned
- Managed
- Marketed
- Maximized
- Mentored
- Merged
- Modified
- Motivated
- Negotiated
- Operated
- Opposed
- Optimized
- Orchestrated
- Organized
- Outsourced
- Oversaw
- Partnered
- Performed
- Pioneered
- Planned
- Positioned
- Possessed
- Powered
- Practiced
- Prepared
- Presided
- Procured
- Promoted
- Proposed
- Protected

Provided
Purchased
Raised
Realigned
Rebuilt
Received
Recognized
Recommended
Redesigned
Reduced
Refinanced
Refined
Regulated
Renegotiated
Reorganized
Repositioned
Represented
Retained

Researched
Resolved
Responded
Restored
Restructured
Revised
Saved
Secured
Selected

Sold
Solidified
Spearheaded
Streamlined
Strengthened
Stretched

Supported
Sustained
Transferred

Transformed
Transitioned
Translated
Utilized
Ventilated
Vetted
Warehoused
Worked

Executive Phrases

- Assessed corporate financial structure
- Asset-based lending facility
- Asset management
- Best practices
- Business development
- Business divestiture
- Business transformation
- Capital acquisition
- Capital restructuring
- Change management
- Competitive product positioning
- Continuous process improvement
- Contract negotiations
- Corporate startup
- Corporate turnaround
- Cost improvement
- Cost rationalization
- Created stakeholder value
- Creditor negotiation
- Crisis management
- Disciplined execution
- Due diligence
- E-commerce licensing
- Equity private placement
- Expense efficiencies
- Financial restructuring
- Global strategies
- High-performance organizations
- Human capital
- Improved bottom-line profitability
- Improved customer experience
- Improved employee engagement
- Improved value proposition
- Increased profitability by percentage
- Key vendor contracts
- Market penetration
- Merger management
- New product/service and technology launch
- Operational readiness
- Organizational alignment
- Organizational efficiency
- Pay for performance incentives
- Positive liquidity
- Pricing strategy
- Quarterly earnings calls
- Raised $X million in new venture funding
- Reduced operating costs
- Significant market opportunities
- Strategic imperatives
- Strategic leadership
- Strategic planning
- Successful IPO
- Succession planning
- Value creation strategies

Professional Talent and Sales Search Action Verbs

Accompanied
Accomplished
Accounted
Acted
Added
Addressed
Administered
Admitted
Advanced
Advised
Advocated
Agreed
Aligned
Allocated
Analyzed
Applied
Assembled
Assessed
Assigned
Assimilated
Assisted
Assumed
Assured
Attained
Audited
Authored
Awarded
Badge
Balanced
Based
Benchmarked
Blended
Bracketed
Branded
Bound
Bridged
Briefed
Buffered
Built
Calculated
Captured
Cared
Carried
Certified
Chaired
Challenged
Championed
Changed
Charted
Clarified
Classified
Cleared
Closed
Coached
Coded
Collaborated
Collected
Combined
Commanded
Compared
Compiled
Completed
Composed
Computerized
Conceived
Conceptualized
Conducted

- Consolidated
- Constructed
- Consulted
- Contributed
- Controlled
- Converted
- Cooked
- Coordinated
- Counseled
- Created
- Customized
- Cut
- Danced
- Deciphered
- Decreased
- Defined
- Delighted
- Delivered
- Demonstrated
- Designed
- Determined
- Developed
- Discovered
- Dispatched
- Displaced
- Disposed
- Distinguished
- Distributed
- Diversified
- Documented
- Doubled/Tripled
- Downsized
- Drafted
- Dreamed/Dreamt
- Drove
- Dug
- Employed
- Enabled
- Endured
- Engaged
- Engineered
- Enhanced
- Established
- Estimated
- Evaluated
- Exceeded
- Expanded
- Extracted
- Facilitated
- Finalized
- Financed
- Finessed
- Forced
- Forecasted
- Found
- Founded
- Functioned
- Gained
- Gathered
- Generated
- Graded
- Graduated
- Grasped
- Grew
- Guided
- Handled
- Heated
- Hired
- Identified
- Ignited

Imaged	Multiplied
Imagined	Networked
Immersed	Obtained
Implemented	Offered
Improved	Opened
Incorporated	Operated
Increased	Opposed
Indicated	Optimized
Initiated	Orchestrated
Injected	Ordered
Integrated	Organized
Introduced	Outperformed
Incubated	Packaged
Invested	Participated
Joined	Performed
Laminated	Piloted
Launched	Pioneered
Leased	Planned
Led (not the metal "lead")	Pointed
Linked	Posted
Listened	Powered
Loaned	Prepared
Located	Presented
Maintained	Presided
Managed	Priced
Manufactured	Prioritized
Marched	Processed
Marketed	Procured
Mentored	Produced
Merchandized	Programmed
Merged	Promoted
Modified	Proposed
Monitored	Prospected
Motivated	Proved
Moved	Provided

- Published
- Punctuated
- Purchased
- Qualified
- Raised
- Rationalized
- Reacted
- Reassessed
- Rebuilt
- Recognized
- Recommended
- Recruited
- Reduced
- Re-engineered
- Reflected
- Remodeled
- Removed
- Repaired
- Reported
- Represented
- Researched
- Restored
- Retained
- Returned
- Revamped
- Reviewed
- Revised
- Revitalized
- Rezoned
- Rinsed
- Sampled
- Saved
- Searched
- Scoured
- Screened
- Secured
- Selected
- Served
- Shortened
- Simmered
- Simplified
- Simulated
- Skilled
- Sold
- Sought
- Sourced
- Specialized
- Spent
- Stirred
- Stored
- Streamlined
- Stretched
- Structured
- Supervised
- Supported
- Sustained
- Targeted
- Tasked
- Teamed
- Terminated
- Tested
- Tracked
- Trained
- Transferred
- Transitioned
- Tuned
- Turned
- Utilized
- Verified
- Warehoused

Weighed
Willed
Wrote

Professional Talent and Sales Phrases

Achieved ambitious goals
Best practices initiatives
Brand awareness
Client focused
Cohesive, cross-functional team
Cold calling
Compensation analysis
Consistently X percent of goal
Consultative selling
Continuous process improvement
Creative client sourcing
Customer penetration
Due diligence
Employee engagement
Exceeded expectations
Execution of concept
Grew territory revenues X percent
Improved client experience by...
Increased growth and profitability
Investment community
Key business metrics
Lead generation
Lean continuous improvement
Long-term company growth
Maintained high employee retention
Market research
Merger and acquisition
Mission critical
Outstanding performance
Performance metrics
Reduced employee attrition
Reported sales metrics
Sales pipeline development
Six Sigma
Solution-based selling
Strategic sales positioning
Strategy development
Working capital

Entry Level Search Action Verbs

Accomplished
Accounted
Achieved
Acquired
Acted
Added
Administered
Admitted

Adopted
Advanced
Advocated
Agreed
Allocated
Analyzed
Applied
Assembled
Assessed
Assigned
Assisted
Assumed
Attained
Attended
Authored
Awarded
Balanced
Branded
Built
Calculated
Capitalized
Captured
Cared
Carried
Certified
Challenged
Championed
Changed
Charted
Checked
Clarified
Classified
Cleared
Closed
Coached
Coded
Collaborated
Collected
Combined
Compared
Compiled
Completed
Composed
Computerized
Conceived
Conducted
Constructed
Consulted
Contributed
Controlled
Converted
Cooked
Coordinated
Corrected
Counseled
Created
Customized
Cut
Danced
Dealt
Deciphered
Decreased
Delighted
Delivered
Demonstrated
Designed
Determined
Developed
Devised
Discovered

- Dispatched
- Displaced
- Distinguished
- Distributed
- Diversified
- Documented
- Drafted
- Drove
- Dug
- Elaborated
- Emphasized
- Employed
- Endured
- Engaged
- Engineered
- Enhanced
- Ensured
- Established
- Estimated
- Evaluated
- Exceeded
- Excelled
- Executed
- Expanded
- Experienced
- Explored
- Facilitated
- Filed
- Financed
- Finessed
- Filled
- Filmed
- Flew
- Followed
- Forecasted
- Formed
- Found
- Founded
- Functioned
- Gained
- Gathered
- Generated
- Graded
- Graduated
- Grasped
- Grew
- Guided
- Hired
- Identified
- Imaged
- Imagined
- Immersed
- Implemented
- Improved
- Incorporated
- Increased
- Indicated
- Initiated
- Injected
- Input
- Instructed
- Integrated
- Interacted
- Interfaced
- Interned
- Interviewed
- Introduced
- Incubated
- Invested
- Joined

Laminated
Launched
Learned
Led
Linked
Listened
Managed
Manned
Marched
Marketed
Modified
Monitored
Motivated
Moved
Multiplied
Negotiated
Obtained
Offered
Opened
Operated
Opposed
Optimized
Orchestrated
Ordered
Organized
Outperformed
Paid
Participated
Partnered
Performed
Piloted
Planned
Pointed
Posted
Practiced
Prepared
Presented
Presided
Prioritized
Processed
Produced
Programmed
Promoted
Proposed
Prospected
Proved
Provided
Published
Punctuated
Purchased
Qualified
Raised
Reacted
Recognized
Recommended
Recorded
Reduced
Reflected
Remodeled
Removed
Repaired
Reported
Represented
Required
Researched
Responded
Restored
Resulted
Returned
Rinsed

- Sampled
- Saved
- Scheduled
- Scoured
- Searched
- Secured
- Selected
- Served
- Serviced
- Shadowed
- Shared
- Shortened
- Simmered
- Simplified
- Simulated
- Sold
- Sought
- Sourced
- Specialized
- Spent
- Spoke
- Stirred
- Stored
- Streamlined
- Structured
- Studied
- Submitted
- Suggested
- Summarized
- Supervised
- Supported
- Sustained
- Targeted
- Taught
- Teamed
- Timed
- Tracked
- Trained
- Transferred
- Transitioned
- Tuned
- Turned
- Understood
- Updated
- Used
- Utilized
- Verified
- Weighed
- Won
- Worked
- Wrote

Entry Level Phrases

Achieved on-time project performance
Participated in (any leadership roles in college like
 sports/clubs/student
government)
Conducted case study on...
Created consensus
Exceeded expectations
Fluent in (foreign languages)
Honor society
Improved customer experience
Learned new work cultures through...
Led team in...
Paid/contributed to college expenses
Participated in industry co-op program
Held part-time college jobs
Completed relevant coursework
Researched...
Strong work ethic as evidenced by...
Student member of (professional association)
Worked in

APPENDIX B

Potential Interview Questions

Entire books have been written that focus solely on interviewing and interviewing questions. The purpose here is not to write a book, but to prepare you for some questions that you may have to field.

Obviously, every interview for every position in every company should be different; however, there are some general questions that may be asked at each level based on that level of experience and responsibility. Most of those questions probably will be self-explanatory. After some questions, I will explain the motivation behind the question.

Review Step 6, "Impressive Interviewing," to see how these different methods of interviewing within the different interviewing formats may be used. Remember the value in telling stories to illustrate your experience and points.

These potential questions are separated by level of experience. Remember, most people conduct interviews without having been trained; therefore, even an executive may be asked a question that targets more junior-level experience because the interviewer may just be going down a list of questions that was handed to her by human resources or a friend. Many questions are developed based on the challenges the candidate will face in the new position.

Some of the questions listed here were taken from actual interviews I have conducted. You can see that I have worked with a wide variety of people.

Use these questions to begin your interview preparation. It is not an exhaustive list, but should get you thinking in the proper frame of mind.

Executive Level Questions

Based on my experience as a recruiter, just when you say, "They will never ask me a question like that. I'm too senior," some interviewer will ask you that question or one like it. Be prepared.

Describe your rise from the staff level to the executive level. What elements do you feel made the difference in your rise to executive level?

Where was luck made?

How do you prepare yourself prior to starting as the leader of a new company?

Do you feel that working in one industry your entire career is more important than successfully working in several industries? Why/why not?

In your current/last position, what do you feel was the most important impact that you made? Why?

What was the most important impact that you made for the investors? What challenges did you have to overcome? As the result of that experience, what did you learn?

Given your understanding of this position and the skills required to be successful, how do you feel your experience may differentiate you from other potential candidates?

Employee 5.0

Using 20/20 hindsight, describe an executive decision that you would have changed had you known then what you know now. *(Ask what level of detail they are looking for. Then tell the story at that level of depth.)*

A leader in a startup has a different role than a leader in a large, mature company or a leader in a corporate restructuring/turnaround. Compare and contrast the different roles these leaders have. Which roles have you filled? Of those roles, which do you prefer? Why?

If you are the leader of a pre-IPO startup, when do you decide to go on the road show to attract new funding? What elements do you feel need to be in place prior to your road show? Who accompanies you on this road show and what are their roles? What is your primary role?

Describe your corporate crisis management experience.

If you are the incoming president/CEO/CFO of a distressed company, what does your first day look like? First week? First month?

What reports do you want to see first? Why?

How often do you communicate with your board the first week and month? When are you confident that you can communicate less often?

Based on your experience and looking forward to the next five years, what situations do you feel would be ideal for you? Why?

There is a lot of talk today about improved productivity among your employees. How do you measure employee engagement? Based on your experience, describe how you improved employee engagement in your last position.

Which industries do you feel can be more profitable in these economic times? Based on your research on our company, what do you feel may be the low-hanging fruit that you will examine first? *(Those questions may be asked in any economic time.)*

What are the sales and marketing roles of the executives in a company this size?

When do you decide to make changes in the sales and marketing leadership roles within your company? Have you changed direction in the past? Were you happy with the result? What did you learn?

When you begin to lead a new company, what legal reports do you want to see first? Have you ever been surprised to find legal problems in a new company? Describe that experience. What did you learn from that experience?

What do you feel is the role of continuous improvement in our industry? Do you feel this company will benefit by instituting a formal continuous improvement program? What pushback do you expect from the current staff?

What do you feel are your best leadership skills? Why? Of those skills, which do you feel will serve you best in this position?

What skills will you need to improve while in this position? What process will you use to improve those skills?

When you are interviewing new members for your team, what do you feel is more important—skill or fit? Why?

How highly do you value human resources in your company? Does your human resource leader meet with your board?

What contribution to the company do you expect from your human resource leadership? Why? Does your current human resource department make that contribution? Why/why not?

What will former executive team members say about their experience working with you? Why?

In what areas do you feel they may suggest you need additional coaching? Why?

What do you feel is the hallmark of your success so far? Why? *(Great time for a story!)*

Obviously, these are general questions that may be asked. You will hear more specific questions based on the needs of the company. The purpose of this list of questions is to help you think about the interview ahead of time.

Professional and Sales Level Questions

Tell me about your experience. *(This question may also be posed as, "Tell me about yourself." This is a great time to use your "Here I Am!" speech that you created in Step 2.)*

What was your last salary? What are you seeking? *(Essentially, both are the same question—trying to determine where you fit within their salary ranges. Remember your salary negotiation script in Step 11? This is an appropriate time to use it.)*

What training have you received from your current employer?

What training have you done on your own? *(Looking to see if you are passionate about what you do.)*

What professional association(s) do you belong to? Does your company pay the dues or do you pay them? *(If you only will belong to an association if your employer pays the dues, how serious are you about your profession?)*

Why are you interested in changing jobs at this time?

What do you like about your current position?

What annoys you at your current company? *(Be careful with your response to this question.)*

Have you ever had a confrontation with a co-worker? Describe the situation. What were your actions? How was the situation resolved?

Typically, at what level of management do you interact?

How do you establish/maintain strong working relationships with company management?

How do you establish/maintain strong working relationships with your peers?

What do you find most helpful in a manager? Least helpful? *(The interviewer should know the style of management of the hiring manager. If your work style and your new manager's work style clash, it will be a poor match for both of you. Be honest.)*

Describe your idea of the best next job for you. *(Be honest. If you say what you feel the manager wants to hear, you may get a job you hate. It's better to know prior to an offer.)*

How does that fit within your long-term goals? *(Actually, they're trying to see if you set goals. Have you thought out where you want your career to head?)*

At what age did you begin to earn money for doing work? *(This could be babysitting or grass cutting.)* Why? *(Work ethic is established early. They are trying to determine your work ethic.)*

In your annual reviews, in what areas do you typically "Exceed Expectations"? Why?

In what areas do you typically fall short of expectations or only meet expectations? Why?

For positions that require driving
(such as sales, consulting, construction or for-hire drivers)

Do you have a valid driver's license with a clean driving record?

Have you ever had your driver's license suspended or revoked? Describe the situation. When was your license reinstated? *(It's best to respond honestly to this question. It's too easy to check during a background investigation. Many insurance companies will not allow employees to drive for business who have poor driving records.)*

Have you ever been convicted of a DUI?

For positions that require travel (consulting, sales, marketing, driving long distances, etc.)

Have you ever traveled more than 50 percent of the time?

Is there anything that would prevent you from traveling overnight more than 50 percent of the time?

What do you like about business travel?

What percentage of overnight travel is acceptable to you?

Technical types of questions (Obviously, a good manager will test your specific technical skills more strenuously!)

Describe your (data network/JD Edwards Development/ Oracle applications/desktop support/web coordinator, software engineering, network engineering, etc.) experience.

What process do you use to troubleshoot technical problems? *(Looking for a step-by-step analysis.)*

What has been your biggest technical challenge? Describe the situation. What were your actions? What were the results? Why was this challenge different than other technical challenges?

What steps do you take to work with an internal client who is upset with the technology or the time to get a new system debugged?

What do you feel are your top five technical strengths with (specific technology)?

What technical skills do you feel you need to improve? How do you plan to improve those skills?

What training has your current employer given you?

Have you ever had to work with users spread out in different states?

How did you support the remote internal clients?

Describe your process to develop credibility with your users when you begin working in a new position or area.

Within your area of expertise, where do you experience the most stress? How do you handle that stress?

Currently, what percentage of your time is spent doing new development vs. maintenance of older systems?
If you are an applications developer, do you prefer SDLC methodology (Waterfall) or Agile methodology (Lean) for software development? Why?

Marketing Questions

Why do you enjoy marketing?

How do you feel sales and marketing feed off each other?

Do you feel it is helpful for a marketing professional to have sales experience? Do you have sales experience? Discuss your experience.

Discuss your brand-development experience.

Discuss your brand-development experience at the channel level.

Have you traveled to clients to learn how to help them make their sales goals with your product (pull-through selling)?

How do you bring value to your company's clients?

Describe your approach to potential clients.

Describe how you developed a marketing-support program.

Have you been a key contributor in the design and implementation of merchandising centers? Discuss one successful implementation.

Discuss your experience in the fulfillment center for the merchandising centers.

What are the key elements in a channel marketing program?

What tasks would you rather other people do in marketing?

Describe the skills and attributes of the perfect vice president of marketing to lead you.

What was your most successful marketing program? Why?

What marketing program do you feel made the largest positive sales gains? Why?

What marketing creative failed? Why? What did you learn? (Even Ford learned through the Edsel failure)

How do you track the success of marketing efforts?

Sales Questions

What was your total compensation?

What was your base?

What was your commission or bonus? *(Sales*

professionals are the one group where I feel compensation should be shared. In my 36 years of recruitment experience, a sales professional typically earns what they believe they can earn. Most sales professionals earn roughly the same amount year after year, adjusted for inflation, unless there has been some life/work-changing event.)

What percentage of goal/quota/target have you made for each of the last four years?

What really turns you on about the sales profession?

What would you rather have someone else handle for you?

How has automation changed your tracking of sales metrics?

Discuss a recent difficult sale that you closed. Why was it unusual? How did you finally close the sale? Is the client currently happy?

How do you normally source for new clients? Describe a recent effort. What was successful? What sourcing effort would you have preferred to be more productive?

While you are conducting needs analysis for a potential client, when are you convinced your solution is the best available?

What do you feel was your best sale? Why?

Describe some of the closes that you have successfully used. Which close has consistently been the most successful?

How do you keep your sales techniques fresh?

What practices do you use to maintain a positive mental attitude?

Describe how you set your goals. For you, what elements are included in a goal?

When do you plan for the week ahead?

How do you plan your day? Week? Month?

How do you define pull-through sales?

Explain the difference between one-step and two-step distribution.

Have you had success in the conceptual sales world? Describe your success. How does conceptual sales differ from product sales?

How do you bring value to your clients?

Describe a creative way you have approached potential clients.

How do you track the success of your efforts in the early months of new business development?

Describe how you were creative in accommodating a difficult client.

What frustrates you? How do you show your frustration?

Project Manager Questions

What do you feel are your strongest project-management skills? How would previous managers describe your project-management skills?

How will your current manager describe your organizational skills?

Many times, to get our jobs done, we are dependent upon others to do their jobs. Give me an example of a time when one of your peers did not have the same priorities as you and was not doing their part. How did you handle that situation? What was the result?

What tool(s) do you use to track project progress?

How do you assign priorities when you are responsible for several projects?

Describe your most difficult project-management assignment. What did you learn from that experience? Have you dealt with a similar experience since?

How do you measure the success of a project? (They are looking for on-time and/or under-budget project that meets requirements.)

Accounting/Audit Questions

What area of accounting is your strength?

Why do you enjoy the accounting profession? (Looking for impacts that can be made.)

Discuss your experience with managerial accounting analysis and reporting.

How strong are your spreadsheet skills? Can you set up a spreadsheet and massage data?

Tell me your experience with standard costs/general ledger/accounts receivable or payable/payroll.

Have you been responsible for manufacturing cost analysis?

Have you been responsible for providing insight for areas of underperformance?

Have you provided sales pricing support for products or services?

Do you have an annual continuous improvement process for standards, inventory and reporting?

Do you have experience with reclaim valuation?

Are you comfortable working and interacting with senior management?

Give an example of a time when you had to convey negative news to senior management. How did you handle negative news to minimize defensiveness and arrive at the best way to remediate?
Describe your group's audit process.

In your current company, how long was your average audit in terms of days/weeks/months?

What percentage of your time is spent in compliance audits, financial audits, operational audits and systems audits?

What audit engagement taught you a valuable lesson? What was the challenge? What was your response? What was the result? What did you learn?

Construction Questions

Have you worked on any infrastructure or commercial or industrial construction sites? What were your responsibilities?

Do you have current safety certifications? Which certifications are current?

What reporting responsibility did you have on a construction site?

Have you ever worked on a wind farm or other renewable-energy construction site? If so, discuss your experience.

What situation best describes your problem-solving skills on a construction site? How was it received by management and other contractors?

How do you initiate and manage change on a construction site?

When you spot work habits that are unsafe, how do you handle the situation?

Describe a situation that was getting out of hand on a construction site. How did you handle it?

How do you convince the person who manages you that you have a better way of doing something? Describe a situation when you used that solution.

What do you feel are your construction management strengths?

What situation best demonstrates your leadership skills on a construction site?

What was the most unusual construction situation that you faced? How did you handle it?

How do you prepare yourself prior to starting on a new construction site? Have you performed safety audits and, as a result, developed new safety programs or policies?

What do you feel you need to learn to be more credible with subcontractors on the construction site? How do you plan to improve those skills?

Human Resource Questions

Describe your experience working in a human resource department.

Typically, what was your most difficult task in human resources? Why?

Describe what you feel are the elements of a human resource business partner. What experience do you need to be a successful business partner? What are you doing to improve those skills?

What training has your company given you to improve your human resource skills?

What human resource training have you sought and paid for on your own?

Do you belong to the Society for Human Resource Management (SHRM)? Does your company pay for your membership? *(Trying to gauge your passion for your profession.)*

What is your process to entertain new ideas to improve human resource processes?

Tell me about a challenging employee issue that you had to handle. Discuss what was the challenge? What was your response? What was the result? What did you learn?

Discuss a manager who was difficult regarding an issue. What was the challenge? What was your response? What was the result? What did you learn?

Describe the worst employee-relations issue that you had to handle. What was the result? Do you feel you handled it in the best possible way? What did you learn?

Discuss your human resource strategy development process for this year. What areas needed process improvement?

Employee 5.0

Discuss a time when you needed to sell senior managers on a new, more expensive (initially) program to improve the business.

Professionally, what would you do a different way if you were given an opportunity to do so? Why?

Discuss a benefits program you introduced that was praised by the employees and saved your company money?

How do you measure employee engagement? How have you improved employee engagement at your current employer?

What element do you feel was most effective in increasing employee engagement?

How did you measure the increase in employee engagement? Who suggested those metrics?

What is your experience in talent acquisition/recruitment? Discuss a situation in which you attracted an impact performer and saved your employer money in the process? *(There are many differing metrics being used here, including integrity.)*

What was your most creative way to source and hire an important employee? How did you decide to employ that process?

In detail, describe the different processes involved in the successful recruitment process.

What applicant tracking/HRIS have you used? Which system do you feel is the best?

Have you successfully sourced candidates through the corporate applicant-tracking system? What do you like about your system? What do you dislike?

What recruitment marketing suggestions have you made for your corporate web site?

Discuss how you best utilize the talents of a third-party recruiter. What do you feel are the challenges of working with a third-party recruiter?

When did you last develop a Recruiting Strategy for the year? Did you complete the year on or over budget? Why?

When we do our reference check, how will the managers that you support describe their experience working with you? Why do you feel we will get that response?

What is your level of compensation analysis experience? Describe the projects that you have completed in this area.

In our reference check, how will your manager describe your strengths and areas of required improvement?

Entry Level Questions

Have you participated in any internships in college?

What was your first internship?

Describe your experience. What kinds of responsibilities did you have?

What did you learn?

What was your biggest adjustment?

What steps did you take to gain acceptance from the full-time staff?

Did they ask you to return for a second internship or offer you a job after graduation?

Would you like to work at that company again as a full-time employee? Why/why not?

Did you work part-time during college? Where? If so, why?

What did you learn?

What benefits do you feel you gained because of your work experience?

What experience in college or work do you feel relates to the skills needed to be successful in this position? *(This is a great time to relate a story about your experience that demonstrates your skills.)*

Did you participate in extracurricular activities in college? Which ones? Why did you pick them?

Did any of your extracurricular activities give you the opportunity to work with a team of other students or professors? What did you learn about working as a team member?

How do you feel you contributed to each of those activities (leadership, ideas, participation in events)?

What would you have done differently?

How do you feel your extracurricular activities affected your GPA?

Looking back, would you have made different choices? Why/why not?

Did you work in high school? Why? *(Work ethic is developed early. This question is trying to determine whether you worked because your parents forced it on you, or you wanted to work for the monetary independence it gave you.)*

When we ask the manager about your work in your high school part time job, what do you think she will say about your work and work ethic? Have you asked for a reference for other jobs or your college application?

What will the manager(s) say about their work experience with you during your summer jobs/internships?

Which professors do you feel would be good references to discuss your work ethic in college? Why? What do you feel they will say to us during a reference check? How do you feel that college prepared you for this position?

Which courses/experiences specifically prepared you for this job?

We realize that few college graduates will move right into a position without needing additional training. After reading the job description, where do you feel we will need to provide you with additional training?

Rate yourself on a scale of 1 to 10 (10 being an experienced Microsoft Office Developer) as a Microsoft Word user. Excel? PowerPoint? Access? How will other classmates rate your experience? How will professors rate you? How will you be rated when we discuss this rating with managers you reported to? *(Hint: Don't rate yourself too highly. Otherwise, you will not be able to meet expectations. Give a brutally honest appraisal after asking the interviewer what a 10 looks like—and tell the interviewer why you rated yourself at this level.)*

Discuss a successful experience that you had while working. Why do you feel it was successful? *(Here is your opportunity to use a story that you developed in the early steps of this book.)* What did you learn from this experience?

Everyone makes mistakes. What mistake did you make that taught you a valuable lesson? What was the challenge? What was your response? What was the result? What did you learn? What would you do differently next time? *(This question is asked to measure your honesty. If you truly never made a mistake, it's time to call the Pope to get you on the fast track to sainthood!)*

Where do you want to make impacts immediately? What experience do you have that will enable you to make those impacts?

Why do you want to work at our company? *(You have been coached to research companies prior to your interview. Companies are aware of that coaching. Now they are testing whether you accept coaching.)*

Have you been in a confrontation with a fellow student? What was the challenge? What was your response? What was the result? What did you learn?

You may use these questions, or some form of them, in the future when you find yourself interviewing candidates for an opening that you are recruiting.

Good luck in your next job! Make it one where you love doing the work SO much, you cannot believe they are paying you!

And Employee 5.0, keep your eye on the horizon for your next great opportunity to grow and contribute!

Acknowledgements

My experience is proof that once you commit yourself to accomplish something and take the necessary actions to be successful, you can succeed. Some people describe that as goal setting.

Thank you to my wife, Linda, and daughters Becky and Sarah. Jason and Ryan are the 2 best sons-in-law that any parent could want for their daughters. Our daughters and sons-in-law have blessed us with two beautiful and intelligent granddaughters, Stori and Zoe. When you have the undying support of loved ones, you can accomplish anything.

Andrea—you have heard me tell many people that you were the best hire I ever made. It is still true. You worked with me through so many false starts on my books and always had great suggestions and supported my ideas. Thank you! Now it's your turn (wink, wink)!

Not to be forgotten are my parents, brothers and sisters. It's really cool how a family comes together and supports one another. Also, they have the relationship to ground you when needed—"Aw, he's just my brother..." Thank you!

Thanks to my teachers and guidance counselor John Moylan at DeMatha Catholic High School in Hyattsville, Md. Three teachers specifically made impacts in my life. Thanks to Father Mike who made biology fun while teaching it. I'll never forget the dead frog that flew out the window and landed on a student's car—I don't think anyone in my class ever parked under Father Mike's window again! Thanks to Buck Offutt who was an English teacher with few peers. Remember the Robin Williams movie when he was the teacher (*Dead Poets Society*)? The movie could have been based on Buck. He taught us not only how to comprehend what we were reading, he taught us to think about what we were reading. Critical thinking is so important in our world! Thanks to Morgan Wootten. Some of you know Morgan as the result of his years of coaching basketball at DeMatha and the fact that he is in the Basketball Hall of Fame (2002). Morgan was my freshman homeroom teacher, my freshman history teacher (Yes, I still remember our project!), and a customer on my *Washington Post* paper route. Morgan taught us values and history—and the importance of not reliving it. He was a better history teacher than he was a basketball coach. Think about it… too bad there is not a History Teacher Hall of Fame!

My professors at Assumption College also contributed to this book because Assumption was my "finishing school." I learned a lot about life at Assumption. Isn't that one of the things you need to learn at that age? John Burke and Michael True were English professors who really made an impact in my life. I gave John a signed copy of my first autographed book before he passed away. He called me to say that I made his day. Thank you, Larry Riordan, the admissions director who recruited me to Assumption and then gave me a work-study job in the admissions office. Who would have thought then that the seeds of my recruiting career were sown?

Be careful if you give a manuscript to Patti Seda, Leadership Coach and Human Capital Consultant at Seda Consulting LLC. She warned me that she loves to use her fine-toothed comb when reading a document. She did. Patti, thank you for your time and suggestions!

A special thanks to Joe Patten. He has been a friend, mentor and client since 1996. His suggestions helped me develop a stronger, more relevant book.

Saving the Best for last—It seems Publishers either get top billing or low billing by authors. Lisa Hagan of Lisa Hagan Books is the Best! Thank you for believing in me and my books!

Beth Wareham—Beth is an Amazing Editor! She provided terrific insights, asked questions that made me think about what I wrote, and was an encouraging mentor. I am looking forward to working with you on future books!

Finally, thank you to God! This book was written to help other people. You helped me with the experience, tools, and extra life as a cancer survivor to help all past and future readers! You kept your promise! Thank you.

—Bill Humbert

NOTES

RecruiterGuy.com Series

NOTES

Employee 5.0

NOTES

RecruiterGuy.com Series

Made in the USA
San Bernardino, CA
07 May 2018